A Better Place To Work

Daily Practices That Transform Culture

Deborah Connors

Published by Well-Advised Publishing, February, 2018
ISBN: 9780995876200

Editor: Danielle Anderson
Typeset: Greg Salisbury
Book Cover Design: Brenda Hewer Design
Portrait Photographer: Landon Sveinson Photography

DISCLAIMER: This book discusses various evidence based practices that have been shown to impact workplace culture in a positive way. As the author states, every culture is different and therefore it is important to tailor each practice to meet the particular needs of your workplace and culture. And even then, the practices you use may need course-correcting as you move forward. The advice and practices herein may or may not be suitable for your situation and the author and publisher will not be liable for any loss of profit or any other personal or commercial damages, including, but not limited to special, incidental, consequential, or other damages. Some of the names and personal characteristics of the individuals involved have been changed in order to disguise their identities. Any resulting resemblance to individuals living or dead is entirely coincidental and unintentional.

FSC
www.fsc.org

MIX
Paper from
responsible sources
FSC® C016245

Printed in Canada

This book is dedicated to the 28 Canadian Workplace Wellness Pioneers. These individuals were nominated and chosen by their peers for their groundbreaking work that has contributed to our understanding about what makes workplaces positive and healthy. We will never fill your shoes, but we can follow in your footsteps.

1997	Kendrith Bentley
	Dr. Martin Collis
	Dr. Ron Labonte
	Russ Kisby
1998	Dr. Roy Shephard
	Dr. Martin Shain
	Murray Martin
1999	Sandy Keir
	Veronica Marsden
	Dr. Art Salmon
2000	Doug Cowan
	Jack Santa-Barbara
2001	Sue Pridham
	Sue Hills
2002	Dr. Linda Duxbury
2003	Joan Burton
2004	Dr. Graham Lowe
2005	Dr. Jean-Pierre Brun
2006	Dr. Derrick Thompson
2007	Nora Spinks
2008	Coreen Flemming
2009	Ed Buffet
2010	Zorianna Hyworon
2011	Mike Ashar
2012	Dr. Ian Arnold
2013	Mary Ann Baynton
	Marion Reeves
2014	Kelly Blackshaw

Gratitude

Some people go away for months to write. Others, like me, fit in minutes between volleyball games and family dinners (thank you Jordan and Jess for the balance in my life), or while travelling back and forth to Alberta in a Ford F150 (thank you Mike for doing all the driving, and for reading all those chapter drafts that I left on your pillow), or in coffee shops in Greece (thank you Mom and Dad for that opportunity to disconnect, vacation and reflect), or dog-sitting in a beautiful house in Ucluelet (thank you Dan and Denise for allowing me that space, and to Charlie the dog for taking me out on walks three times a day) and in hotel rooms while on speaking trips to share this content (thank you to my remarkable clients that make that possible). It takes longer to write this way, but the work is better for the reflection that comes between the spurts of writing.

When I led The Better Workplace Conference for the last time in 2013 (what a great celebration that was!) and I thought back over the 17 years of how this event evolved from the original Health Work & Wellness Conference in 1997, I knew there was a book to be written. It was going to be about the ideas that were shared at the conference over the years that needed to reach a larger audience. I am extremely grateful to the over 600 speakers who shared their stories at Health Work & Wellness/The Better Workplace Conference between 1997-2013. Your messages made a difference to creating awareness about the need for healthier and more positive workplaces in this country. Thank you. All your names are listed in the Resources section.

As I started to write, I took a course with Carla Rieger that helped me to peel back the layers and get to the core of what I had to offer to the world. Thank you Carla! Later, I took an online course with Patti Digh called Organizing Your Writing Life, which was not at all about getting my files in order, but all about what blocks us from writing (which is never about having a messy office!). Thank you, Patti, for the inspiration to develop writing rituals.

Knowing nothing about the publishing industry, I took another online course with Julie Salisbury of Influence Publishing and learned how complex and ever-changing this industry is. Thank you to Julie, who became my partner in publishing this book, and to Greg Salisbury for typesetting and to Danielle Anderson for her great editing.

Over the course of creating chapter after chapter, many others faithfully read each version and provided feedback—thank you to Pat McCue and Shonagh McRae, and also to Rixta Moritz and Hugh Culver for the extra feedback on a few chapters.

Most importantly I am grateful for the organizational health experts from around the world that agreed to in-depth interviews and willingly shared their wisdom and their brave and inspiring stories, some very personal and painful, so that others can learn and benefit: Dr Martin Shain, Dr. Graham Lowe, Dr. Linda Duxbury, Dr. Robert Quinn, Mary-Lou MacDonald, Mary Ann Baynton, Dr. Michael West, Melissa Barton, Dr. Gregor Breucker and Marie Mac Donald.

Thank you to Thoughtexchange for providing the platform for me to hold an online conversation with the organizational health community in Canada and beyond to gather feedback on positive organizations and what leaders need to move in that direction.

In the early years of the conference we realized we needed a good photographer onsite to capture the excitement, the connections and the fun being had. Some of those pictures are included in the center of the book. Thank you to my friend Gottfried Mitteregger for showing up for all those first years, and my nephew, Landon Sveinson, for taking over this role for the final few years. You are both so good at capturing the essence of what is happening at an event, and bringing out the spirit in each person you photograph.

Since the beginning of the conference, we worked with only one designer on our brochures, logos and onsite materials. Thank you Brenda Hewer for your excellent work over the years, and for designing the book cover and many of the diagrams throughout.

And of course, this book never would have been written if the conference never happened, so I am grateful to that first core team who said "Yes!" to this event! Thank you to Sheron Stone, Jeanie Cloutier and Muneerah Kassam—it was a privilege to work with you! Over the 17-year span of this event, there were hundreds of people involved and I cannot thank you all here, but please know that I remember all of your faces, your names and the spirit you brought to this event. I do want to particularly thank: Jonathan Buchwald, Dal Palmer and the great team at PRIME, Andrea Mau, Alison Infante, Marischal de Armond and the team at De Armond Management, Marta Devellano and Jamie Millar-Dixon.

And finally, thank you to Mary Ann Baynton, Great-West Life Assurance Company and the Great-West Life Centre for Mental Health in the Workplace for how you have demonstrated to the country the need for healthy organizations through your support of the conference over the years and your support of this book.

Contents

Definitions

Appreciative Inquiry (AI): a worldview that assumes that every human system has something that works right. AI begins by identifying the positive core and connecting to it in ways that heighten energy, sharpen vision, and inspire action for change. (from The Center for Appreciative Inquiry)

Bilingual Leadership: possessing both transformational leadership and conventional management skills and knowing when to use each. (Dr. Robert Quinn, 2015)

Careful Workplace: one that conserves individual, social and economic capital by causing no foreseeable physical or psychological harm to individuals. (Dr. Martin Shain, 2017)

Compassionate Leadership: paying close attention to all staff and really understanding the situations they face, and then responding empathetically and taking thoughtful and appropriate action to help. Compassionate leadership includes four main qualities: attending, understanding, empathizing and supporting. (from Dr. Michael West, The King's Fund, UK)

Culture: patterns of social behaviour and normative expectations that become characteristic of an organization's functioning, without its members consciously choosing them. (Robert F. Allen, 1987)

Culture Shift: consciously shifting the culture of your organization, typically aiming for a more positive psychological and social environment.

Emergent Process: Robert Quinn defines emergence as when "something appears, occurs, or materializes without direction and control from the top." Learning to trust the emergent process is one of the principles of positive organizing.

Emotional Intelligence (EI): the ability to recognize and handle our own emotions and those of others. It is generally said to include three skills: emotional awareness, the ability to harness emotions and apply them to tasks like thinking and problem solving, and the ability to manage emotions, which includes regulating your own emotions and cheering up or calming down other people. (from Psychology Today)

Flourishing: living within an optimal range of human functioning, one that connotes goodness, generativity, growth and resilience. (Frederickson and Losada, 2005)

Focused Writing: writing off the top of your head with no judgement; just setting a timer and writing whatever comes to mind, with no rules. If you can't think of anything to say, just write "I can't think of anything to say" until something comes. The idea is to keep your pen moving for a specified period, and to let your thoughts flow through your pen. (Adapted from Patti Digh, Life is a Verb, 2008)

Leader: someone who has a vision and changes the culture of a system to make it better. (Robert Quinn)

Inter-Team Working: Dr. Michael West defines "Inter-team cooperation" as the effectiveness of the team in working with other teams in the organization with which it has to work in order to deliver products or services. (Michael West, 2012)

Mindfulness: paying attention on purpose, in the present moment, and non-judgmentally. (Jon Kabat-Zinn, 1994)

Mindlessness: being unaware of what is going on around us and/or how we are responding to it. (Ellen Langer, 1989)

Organizational Health: a "way of doing business" which includes effective communication, dynamic leadership, healthy workplace culture, decision latitude, work and family policies and practices and effective change leadership. It is a mindset that permeates the organization—that encourages creativity, innovation, productivity and diversity of ideas. It is a culture that celebrates personal responsibility for well-being and supports employees to be their best physically, mentally, socially, spiritually and emotionally. Most companies have many of the components listed above, but it is the integration of these aspects with each other and into the way business is conducted that creates a healthy organization. (derived from Deborah Connors message in the Health Work & Wellness Conference brochure, 1998)

Positive Deviance: intentional behaviors that depart from the norms of a referent group in honorable ways. (Spreitzer and Sonenshein, 2012)

Positive People Culture: a culture where people experience positive emotions, optimism, cohesion, gratitude and humour, and where they have as a consequence, a real sense of engagement. (Dr. Michael West)

Positive Organization: a system in which the people flourish and exceed expectations. (Robert Quinn, 2015)

Practice: engaging in an activity again and again, in an attempt to improve it.

Possibility Thinking: broadening our minds to see the possibilities versus simply focusing on constraints. (adapted from the work of both Barbara Fredrickson and Robert Quinn)

Resilience: positive adaptation, or the ability to maintain or regain mental health, despite experiencing adversity. (Sage Journals)

Senior Executive: someone with positional authority; someone at the top of the hierarchy.

Slow Death: a situation that arises in organizations when we disengage from what is good for the organization to pursue our own interests, and when we ignore signs that our strategies are ineffective, leading to feelings of hopelessness throughout the organization. (Quinn, 2012)

Transformational Leadership: Transformational leaders are those who can effectively improve culture, typically through a focus on vision versus problem solving. (Quinn, 2012)

Wellness: a high state of physical, psychological, emotional, spiritual and social well-being.

360-Degree Assessment: [this] refers to the practice of involving multiple raters, often including self-ratings, in the assessment of individuals. Typically, feedback about a target individual is solicited from significant "others," using a standardized assessment instrument. These "others" typically include the individual's co-workers, subordinates, and managers, as well as customers. The requirement is that they are knowledgeable about the individual and are people whose opinions are valued by the individual and the organization. (onlinelibrary.wiley.com)

Introduction

"There are two primary choices in life; to accept conditions as they exist, or accept the responsibility for changing them."
—Denis Waitley

Something magical happened in the fall of 1997. If you were one of the 550 people who walked into the Hotel Vancouver for the very first Health Work & Wellness™ Conference in Canada, you will know exactly what I'm talking about.

The energy and excitement was palpable. There had never been a forum of this kind in the country, and people with different backgrounds from workplaces across the nation and beyond came to be a part of the inaugural event. The fact that the delegates were not from just one profession or one industry is what made the atmosphere so electric.

We started this conference because we thought there was a better way to do business, and apparently those 550 people thought so too. Right from the get-go we were focusing on organizational culture as the key to building a better workplace, but not everyone was ready to hear that message yet.

The opening keynote speaker at that first conference was workplace health expert and professor Dr. Ron Labonte. He opened with a talk about the social determinants of health in the workplace, covering concepts like control, respect, trust, flexibility and communication.

In the elevator after his opening address, I asked a woman (who did not know I was the founder of the event), "What did you think of Dr. Labonte's talk?" This question brought forth a rant about how "this is not what wellness is all about!" Her vision of a healthy workplace did not encompass shifting the culture. It was about programs, checklists and "best practices," and Labonte's presentation clearly did not fit into her world view.

My thought was, *Good! He's created some controversy here, so now we can open up some real conversation!* Because at that time, most people were pre-occupied with personal health practices and programs that dealt with smoking cessation, stress management and fitness. All very worthy projects, but unlikely to create the kind of positive and healthy psychological environment necessary for people to flourish at work and contribute their best.

This book is the story of the conversations and innovations that were shared at the Health Work and Wellness™ Conference (which later became branded as The Better Workplace Conference) over the 17 years that I led the event. In that period, we brought together innovators and influencers from around the world who were studying and leading positive change, both inside their organizations and with their clients. Through running this event, I had the unique opportunity to meet and get to know hundreds of incredible thought-leaders and keynote speakers. Ten of these influencers who I was particularly inspired by agreed to be interviewed for this book, and their stories and advice can be found within these pages.

This powerful conference also attracted a community of like-minded individuals and created a whole generation of workplace health and wellness professionals. As part of my research for this book I reached out to this community to start a conversation on positive workplace culture, and have included their thoughts and stories as well.

As organizational health has evolved in Canada, the awareness and understanding about this concept has changed. Just as Labonte suggested all those years ago, it is very clear that creating a better place to work starts with shifting the culture. There are some good news stories of positive and lasting change, but there are also accounts of those who have tried new ways, failed, and learned great lessons in the process. These stories have been gathered here as inspiration for those of you who are striving for a more positive culture at work.

Collectively, the stories show that shifting the culture in your workplace, whether you are an organization of one or ten-thousand-and-one, is not as much about policies, strategies and programs (although these are all helpful) as it is about practices—daily applications that you can start putting in place immediately.

Some of these practices are individual ones that we, as leaders, can begin today, such as learning how to replace the vicious cycles we get into with resilient ones. Others, such as team debriefs, can be used to improve the effectiveness of our teams. And some, such as the practice of positive organizing, can be used with large groups and organizations. You can implement these changes from anywhere within your organization; it doesn't have to start at the top.

A profound way to begin to shift your culture is to find the transformational question that will help you to think differently, help your team to take on a new challenge, or help your organization to get engaged in a new vision. I have used transformational questions in each chapter, and the one that forms the through-line for this book is simply:

> What will we do differently to create a better place to work?

I urge you to keep this question in mind as you work through this book. Just as there is no step-by-step process to creating positive culture change, there is no prescribed order to reading this book. Start anywhere. Read the stories and recommendations. Ask yourself the questions as you go, and then ask them of your teams. Take notes in your journal, or write in the margins of this book. Work through the activities and practices in each chapter. Highlight things that jump out at you. And, most importantly, tailor them to fit your own situation. The book was designed to be a practical guide that you can apply immediately in your place of work.

At the core of a great workplace is leadership from all levels. In order to pursue the best possible future for our organizations, we need to take the lead and move out of our comfort zone, learn new ways of doing things, empower people to step into possibility and positivity, and let the future transpire through us.

Inspiring examples and stories are everywhere; you can find them sprinkled throughout the pages of this book. There are courageous leaders who are asking their people what they want their culture to be. There are transformational leaders inspiring their employees to see possibility.

Immerse yourself in these powerful, positive stories; engage your teams in the change process; declare your vision and commitment as a leader to transform your culture; ask the right questions and trust what will emerge.

Grab a cup of coffee, a pen and a highlighter, and enjoy the process as you read, write and work your way into some new positive practices!

CHAPTER 1

"The bad times won't last forever, but the story of how you stood up to them will. It's time to write that story."
—**Stan Slap, Keynote Speaker, Conference 2010**

I'm sitting in the chair at a new hair studio and, making conversation, the stylist asks me what I do. When I tell him that I teach leaders how to radically shift culture so that people can flourish, he says, "Oh, do we ever need that here!" It's a familiar theme, whether I'm at the dentist, the accountant or talking to someone at a networking event. Invariably, when the topic of creating a better place to work comes up, people have a lot to say. It usually goes something like, "Business is great, but…" and then they go on to say something negative about the social environment at work. It's often related to feeling overwhelmed or undervalued.

Why does this topic come up repeatedly? I think it is because as these businesses or departments grow and change, nine times out of ten, there is a focus on the core business, the products, the sales and marketing strategies and even on the customer experience, but no thought is given to the people doing the work.

A person's performance at work is largely tied to whether they feel supported and appreciated by their organization. Hal Rosenbluth said it best in his book "The Customer Comes Second": "Only when people know what it feels like to be first in someone else's eyes can they sincerely share that feeling with others."[1]

Yet I have seen many small businesses make the mistake of doing whatever it takes to please the client, at the expense of their own staff. Many departments within big organizations implement technical changes without having a strategy to help their people manage the effects of those changes on their mental and emotional health. People are then left feeling overwhelmed, stressed, burned out, and less able to be creative and to contribute their best work.

In preparation for this book I gathered information on healthy workplace culture, reviewing research from the thought-leaders I brought together over the 17-year period of leading The Better Workplace Conference, formerly called the Health Work & Wellness™ Conference. Because of the change in names, I will be referring to this event simply as "the Conference" for the remainder of the book.

I conducted in-depth interviews with ten particularly inspiring experts: Dr. Robert Quinn, Dr. Martin Shain, Dr. Michael West, Dr. Linda Duxbury, Marie Mac Donald, Dr. Graham Lowe, Melissa Barton, Mary-Lou MacDonald, Dr. Gregor Breucker, and Mary Ann Baynton.

This compilation of expert advice leads us to one conclusion: if we change our culture, we change our outcomes. Although programs, strategies and policies support conditions where people can flourish and succeed, it is the culture (or "how we do things around here") that creates those conditions. Flourishing people contribute their best, see more possibilities, and are more proactive and innovative. If your change effort does not address the culture, success in achieving organizational health will be minimal.

The late Robert F. Allen describes culture (which he calls the "organizational unconscious"), as being "those patterns of social behaviour and normative expectations that become characteristic of an organization's functioning, without its members consciously choosing them." He describes how unconscious activity can block our conscious goals, so the first step in shifting those unconscious behaviours is recognizing them.[2]

Once we know that these behaviours and norms exist, they can be consciously improved. This positive improvement to the culture happens through the practices or behaviors we partake in daily. To "practice" means to engage in an activity repeatedly in order to improve it. For example, as we practice active listening, over time we become better listeners and can pick up on more verbal and non-verbal cues.

A practice is something that is never "mastered." For example, as I practice examining my hypocrisies as a leader, I may get better at leading by example. However, will I get to a point where there is no hypocrisy between what I do and what I say? Probably not; there are always opportunities for further improvement.

As you will see throughout this book, there is overwhelming evidence that we can increase positivity and resilience in people, teams and organizations through daily practices. These practices positively impact creativity, innovation, productivity, employee satisfaction, customer service, customer satisfaction and the financial outcomes of the organization.

All too often though, efforts to improve organizational health focus only on implementing a program. This might be a stress management program or a series of lunch and learn seminars. While the information in these programs may be useful, the focus is on individual health, not the health of the organization and—more specifically—not on changing the culture. In fact, the culture is often not even considered as the reason for the lack of organizational health or performance. The culture does not change with this approach, and research shows that most workplace health programs yield poor results in terms of their impact on organizational performance.

Here's a mini practice for you: each time you see one of these questions in a box throughout the book, put the book down and think about how it would feel to ask this question in your workplace. There is a question posed in each chapter, like the one below, that I hope will be a transformational one for you—one that makes you think differently, take on a new challenge or create a new vision. It will be in a green, abstract box somewhere in the chapter. When you come across each one, stop and reflect on it and perhaps make a few notes for yourself.

> How will your workplace be different
> tomorrow if there is a positive shift today?

If you look ahead six months, what differences would you like to see in your workplace? What about one year from now? Three years from now?

The goal of this book is to help you achieve this vision. It will encourage you to shift your culture in an upward direction by developing practices that increase your positivity and resilience and help you to become a more transformational leader. Doing this work will greatly increase your chance of creating a culture where people can contribute their best.

Slow Death

If we are doing nothing to move our organization in a positive direction, it will be spiraling towards what Dr. Robert Quinn calls "slow death."

Quinn was the opening keynote speaker at the Conference in 2012. He is author of several outstanding books on leadership and positive workplaces.[3,4] He is also one of the thought-leaders I interviewed for this book.

In his decades of studying organizations, he has observed that they are always in the state of becoming more positive or becoming more negative; they are never stagnant. The "normal" state is to grow, and then to plateau. At this point, things become routine and people tend to get comfortable and, often, complacent. The problem is that the world outside the organization is not stagnant, and so what may feel like maintenance is the start of a downward spiral leading to slow death.

You may have experienced this circumstance at some point; I personally encountered it when working in a large organization where the culture seemed to get more and more negative. People were burning out, but no one seemed to know how to stop the decline. This is a common phenomenon, and is sometimes the result of not wanting to—or not knowing how to—make the deep changes needed to turn things around.

Quinn says that most people choose slow death over making deep change. Why? Because shifting the culture requires significant personal change, and this often seems daunting.

There is no step-by-step, cookie-cutter approach to this challenge. Quinn describes North American organizations as having a "checklist mentality," meaning we want an easy path (or checklist) to follow. It often looks like this: an expert comes up with a strategy that works in one organization, which then becomes a "best practice" which others copy. It is a fast and easy process, but one that doesn't often work because every workplace culture will respond differently to a set approach.

To illustrate this checklist mentality, Quinn talks about the great success that Toyota had years ago with their Lean Program.[5] Lean is a method of maximizing customer value while minimizing costs. Thousands of companies have tried to replicate what Toyota achieved, but only a few have been successful. Quinn believes this is because the best implementation of the model is about changing the way people think and act at work rather than simply copying an existing strategy verbatim.

When it comes to organizational health and wellness, most companies take the same approach. A high percentage of large organizations will report having a wellness program which may include fitness, mental health, disease management or any number of health initiatives. In most cases, this program does not address the workplace culture.

In my interview with Dr. Quinn, he said, "Many administrators don't even see the culture, or understand it, much less imagine changing it. Most don't see culture as their business."

Many senior executives see managing the culture as someone else's job.

Maybe you're the "someone else."

The Cost of Doing Nothing

Culture is not always seen as being important to business goals. However, there is a "cost to doing nothing." This is a phrase often used by Dr. Martin Shain, an organizational health and legal expert who has studied the implications of negative psycho-social environments at work. He was a keynote speaker at some of our earlier conferences, and when I interviewed him I asked him about this. He replied:

> *The cost of doing nothing refers to the fact that nothing is ever neutral – things are either going forward or going backwards, so if you're doing nothing, things are basically going backwards.*
>
> *Those costs are measurable and quantifiable, so you can use them as the baseline for moving forward. But if you don't do anything, things are much more likely to get worse than to get better.*

The choices we make every day shape the story of our workplace. What is the story you're writing in yours? Perhaps you see a need for a radical shift in your culture. Perhaps you've been through bad times, and you're the one pushing to make work a better life experience for everyone.

Whatever your motivation, what's important for you to know is that you have the power to create a better place to work.

That's right. You.

The magnitude of that change will depend more on your sense of power and purpose than it will on your position in the organization. Anyone at any level can be a leader; positional authority does not equate to leadership. Most of the experts I interviewed for this book were very passionate about that point. For example, Dr. Robert Quinn said, "Most executives, including CEOs, are not leaders. Being at the top of the hierarchy doesn't make you a leader. A leader changes the culture of the system and makes the system better."

Dr. Linda Duxbury, who was the keynote speaker at the Conference in 2011, also states, "We confuse positional authority with leadership. A CEO is only a manager if he or she is not leading. Leadership is having a vision and having followers."

Leadership is about seeing where your organization needs to go and taking your people in that direction. Leadership is changing the culture of the system and making it better. In this book, when I use the word "leader" I am referring to people who have a vision and shift the culture for the better. I will call the people with positional authority "senior executives."

This book is for influential leaders who want to improve their workplace culture. It is about how to be "positively deviant" at work—moving away from the normal way of doing business for beneficial reasons.

Flourishing versus Languishing

In positive psychology, flourishing is defined as living "within an optimal range of human functioning, one that connotes goodness, generativity, growth, and resilience."[6]

Positive culture shift happens through daily practices that promote flourishing. These are evidence-based practices that any leader can develop in order to start an upward spiral in their own life, their team, their department or throughout their entire organization.

The practices relate to how we treat each other, how we communicate, how mindful we are throughout our day, our awareness of how we impact others, the integrity with which we work, how and when we disconnect from work, how we find gratitude in our day, and how emotionally intelligent we are. They disrupt downward spirals in order to create environments where individuals, teams and organizations can thrive.

Diagram #1 shows a simple picture of the organizational benefits of flourishing as well as the negative effects of languishing. Evidence shows that the more positive emotions we experience, the more we tend to flourish. Conversely, the more negative emotions we experience, the more we tend to languish.[7]

For example, the downward spiral of being overextended and exhausted often leads to burnout. Quinn points out that when an employee is in this state, they are also underutilized: their busyness and overwhelm is keeping them from contributing their best. In this situation, there is an organizational and personal "cost to doing nothing."

DIAGRAM #1
Organizational Impact of Flourishing vs Languishing

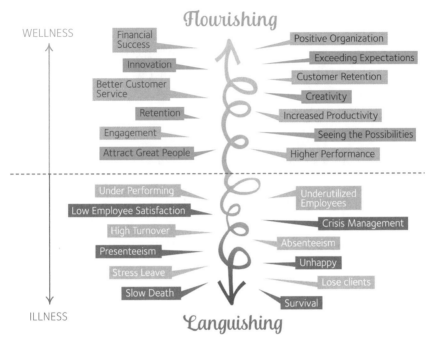

On the other hand, the upward spiral represents what happens when we experience more positive emotions at work. Research shows that this leads to increased creativity, innovation, engagement and flourishing. For example, a work culture that promotes continuous renewal, positivity and resilience leads to better performance outcomes by creating a culture of contribution where people exceed expectations.

Throughout this book, I share over 50 evidence-based, positive practices that can be tailored to fit the culture in your workplace. These are practices that increase positivity, shift focus from downstream to upstream, build resilience, strengthen teams, create learning organizations, set the foundation for psychological health and transform cultures. They will help you shift your culture into an upward spiral, which is important for innovation, performance, attraction, retention, productivity, engagement, and great customer service—all outcomes that any business strives for. In each chapter I will introduce you to new practices and how they can benefit your workplace, but you can also find a summary of these practices in the Resources section at the end of the book.

The key to success in implementing new practices is to tailor and mold each practice to fit your team or workplace.

Stories

I asked every expert I interviewed for a story of positive change in order to provide real-life examples of personal, team, and organizational change and influence. This first one is a story of my own; perhaps you have lived a story like this one.

When I was in my twenties I was hired on a contract to launch a new provincial initiative, and I was excited for this opportunity. I had a good education and a lot to contribute to the organization, and when I started the job it seemed like a great place to work.

As time passed, however, I began noticing some negative patterns. I witnessed inappropriate behavior by those in senior positions, and I saw a lot of people come and go. When an employee had any kind of issue, there was no human resources department to call on. I started to count, and soon realized that employee turnover was about 50% annually. No one in a senior position viewed this as a problem.

But still, I thought I could excel here. I was offered a promotion that held more earning potential, and I was eager to take this on. My director took me aside and advised me to negotiate the best salary I could going in, as raises were not given readily. On his recommendation, I sat down with the Executive Director to discuss my salary expectations. Then I waited. And waited. A few days later, my director gave me a newspaper ad to review before they placed it in the paper. It was for the job I had been offered! Without any explanation, the position was advertised and given to someone outside the organization who no doubt had a lower salary expectation. I asked the Executive Director what happened, but I was never given an answer.

Wait a minute though! Did you notice the circle of communication here? My director coached me to ask for a higher salary, and then the job was taken away *because* I asked for a higher salary? There was a definite lack of clarity and authentic communication.

Shortly after this, I joined the 50% of my colleagues who left the organization every year, and I wrote a letter to the Board of Directors as my own form of an exit interview. Of the twelve board members, I received a phone call from only one. He indicated that he had been concerned about the turnover for some time; as far as I know, that is the extent of the investigation into this issue.

Being a young employee with expectations of fairness and integrity in the workplace, I found the whole experience appalling. It made me think, *There has to be a better way to do business.*

This thought is what made me start and lead the Conference for 17 years. It's my "WHY." It's why I spent the past 30+ years devoting my work to creating better workplaces. It is why I wrote this book.

A Community Thoughtexchange

While I was running the Conference, a community formed. It started as a forum for sharing ideas between organizations across Canada and a way to bring together thought-leaders from around the world. Over time, it became a community of like-minded individuals who were looking for ways to create more positive and healthy workplaces.

As I was pulling together resources for this book, I reached out to this community—one made up of senior executives, organizational health experts, researchers, consultants, managers, directors, human resources professionals and other change agents from a wide array of industries—to hold an online discussion about positive workplace culture. The information I received from this exchange is what guided my questions in the subsequent interviews with the experts.

This discussion was held in partnership with a company called Thoughtexchange. The Thoughtexchange Group Insight Platform™ describes their process in this way: "Rather than simply surveying people, Thoughtexchange lets you ask open-ended questions in a way that lets everyone say all they need to say; everyone learns about tradeoffs that have to be made, and realistic solutions emerge." It is a way of taking the pulse of what those working with these issues are currently thinking.

A Thoughtexchange has three steps: The Share step, where participants are asked up to four very simple, open-ended questions; the Star step, where participants are shown the thoughts of others and can assign stars to the ones they value most; and the Discover step, where participants are invited to view the report and see what themes emerged. In the Share step, we asked four open-ended questions:

1. How do you characterize a positive workplace culture?
2. What practices have you experienced (or heard of) that have improved workplace culture?
3. What are some things that prevent your workplace from achieving a positive workplace culture?
4. What would you like to learn about as a leader interested in improving workplace culture?

151 participants shared 598 thoughts as a part of this conversation. Here are some of the thoughts that really stood out for me. This first thought reinforces the importance of culture and highlights the big picture:

"I enjoy a great workplace culture. People are emotionally intelligent and make a sincere effort to recognize and support others. **When we take on too many projects, however, the demands on our time and energy reduce our ability to be thoughtful in all of our interactions.**"

There was a great deal of discussion around how essential it is to have a positive culture, and about how scheduling and workload can undermine this intent. As our workplaces become more connected through technology, this is increasingly important. These two quotes from the discussion highlight the importance of scheduling and workload:

"**Technology increases the rapidness of work and escalates work expectations and demands—often creating an 'always on' mentality.** People need to be able to separate work from other aspects of their lives to ensure a positive, healthy balance."

"**Staff keep trying to succeed while suffering burnout, which means less ability to get things done.**"

In response to the question about what people want to learn, there were many thoughts shared about learning how to influence change from whatever level they are at. A couple of these are shared below:

"**How to be influential.** It's important because if it's possible to have even a slight opportunity to contribute to a positive workplace culture, I want to do that."

"**How can we influence change even if overall the organization is not ready?**"

What I found most interesting was the request to learn more about stories and storytelling. Participants asked to hear stories of change— real examples of success and culture shift in firms of all sizes. But not only are they eager to hear stories, they also expressed an interest in learning to tell stories, as expressed by one participant:

"We are drowning in data and information overload. **To cut through that clutter we need to become good storytellers.** Stories can convey a theme, an idea, a vision, a desire in ways that data and bureaucratic/corporate speak cannot. Learn to listen and tell stories that matter."

I took this thought to heart and am using my own stories, as well as the stories of the influencers I interviewed, to showcase practices that are contributing to better work.

After looking at the results of this Thoughtexchange, I compiled the main ideas that jumped out at me and will be further expanded on throughout this book:

1. **People generally want to contribute.** This is what we hire them for—their education, expertise, knowledge, experience and what they can contribute to our organizations. They want to exceed our expectations and feel valued. We all want to be in a work situation where we can be creative and innovative, and where we're not overloaded. We want balance and flexibility. We want to have control over where and how we work, to be evaluated by what we contribute and not by how many hours we work. We want to use the skills and talents we were hired for. We want to be happy and have fun at work. In short, we want "great work."[8]

2. **A focus on becoming more positive means shifting focus from downstream to upstream thinking.** Our current focus on organizational health mainly follows the medical model, which

is a problem-solving, treatment-focused approach. Instead, we should be using an upstream or preventive approach.

3. **Leaders model the positive behaviors that begin to shift the culture,** and they engage their teams in creating the vision of "what we want our culture to be" and "who we are when we are at our best."

4. **There is no step-by-step checklist approach to this work.** Although cookie-cutter or program approaches are the easiest to implement, they are rarely successful. What works is tailoring positive, healthy practices to fit your organization or team.

5. **There are evidence-based practices that increase our positive emotions as individuals and teams, and create conditions for organizing positively.** This allows us to see more possibilities and be more productive.

6. **Moving from a conventional management approach to a transformational leadership approach** will lead to more success. This is difficult because conventional management principles are ingrained in us. Transformational leadership focuses on vision versus problem-solving, pays attention to asking questions versus having all the answers, and engages people in purpose, possibilities and the common good.

7. **There are practices that increase our resilience** as individuals, teams and organizations, which results in sustaining great work.

8. **The path will not be clear cut; it will be murky.** Course correction along the way will be necessary. This is how we become learning organizations.

9. **There are many great tools** recommended by the thought-leaders in this book that will help you in your quest for a more positive, healthy culture in your organization.

On the note of great work, I heard Michael Bungay-Stanier speak at the Conference in 2014. He talked about three different types of work—great work, good work and bad work—and then asked us to draw a pie chart and divide it based on how much of each we were doing at the time. Great work is the stuff that feeds your soul, where you're doing what you love; it's meaningful and you feel like you're making an impact. Good work is productive time that uses your talent and education and is interesting. Bad work is that soul-sucking, time-wasting, "busy work," which he says most organizations generate a lot of.

In my interview with Dr. Graham Lowe, professor emeritus at the University of Alberta, he said that great work is what people desire. They want to feel that they are contributing to something larger rather than just getting paid at the end of the week. In his latest co-authored book, "Redesigning Work: A Blueprint for Canada's Future Well-Being and Prosperity," survey data is shared from the early 2000's as well as post-recession. Lowe says,

> *It is clear that there is a real premium that people place on quality work where they can contribute. There are several things that fit together—making a difference, being recognized for it, feeling like you are part of a team or supportive group, and liking the people you work with. Pay is important to people, but pay does not trump any of those other things.[9]*

The "Be Positive" Framework for Shifting Culture

Diagram #2 provides a framework I developed to outline over 50 daily practices that support creativity, innovation and pro-activity at work for individuals, teams and organizations. Each letter in the framework corresponds with a different set of practices, and also with each chapter of this book.

DIAGRAM #2
Framework for a Positive People Culture

Better Way **Engage in Practices**

POSITIVELY DEVIANT

Organize Positively

Shift Yourself 1st

Ignite Positivity

TEAMS

Inspire
Psychological Health

VISION

Emergent Process

The Through-Line Approach to Implementing Practices

I had been skiing for 20 years when I took a lesson that made all the difference to my performance, and not just on the slopes. The instructor talked to us about the "fall line" of the mountain. This is the direction water will flow when it is free to run. When you stand at the top of a mogul run, you can visualize what would happen if you tipped over a bucket of water and watched where it went. There can be any number of paths, but they all follow this fall line. *"When you miss the fall line as a skier you feel as though you are fighting against the mountain, but when you get it right, gravity helps the skis turn and its magic!"*

From the top of the mountain you won't be able to see that line all the way to the bottom—you only see the beginning of it, and you can pick your first three turns. It's mid-course, in real time as you're flying down the mountain, that you pick the next three, and then the next. Often I'll miss a turn and then I'm course correcting on the fly, but I'm always looking for that fall line to follow.

There is a similar concept in acting and writing. It is called the "through-line," and it is the thread or theme that connects the thoughts and concepts. This is what keeps the audience engaged. While the speaker or author may tell many stories or explain different concepts, they always come back to the through-line. In turn, this brings the listener or reader back to the theme or general message they are trying to convey.

We can use this through-line approach when trying to create positive change. It helps immensely to have a vision to work towards (e.g. what do we want our culture to be?), but once we have that the next question is "what are three turns I can take to move toward that vision?"

As a skier, I know what my vision is—to get to the bottom of the run! To do that, my focus needs to be on finding the fall line through the moguls. What are my first three turns? If my focus is on the bottom of the hill, I'm quite likely to tumble rather than ski down because I'm not focused on what is directly in front of me. I need to have a laser focus on what my skis are doing, and when I miss a turn because it is icier or stickier than I thought I need to immediately adjust to the new reality and pick the turn that will get me back on that fall line.

It may seem unnerving not to know what will come after those first three turns, but that's how life is. We want to know all the steps when we're moving through a change and be able to check off the boxes. We are more comfortable with cookie-cutter approaches and following best practices than we are with finding the possibilities and trusting the emergent process. But when we are working toward a more positive or healthy culture at work, it is leadership practices that create change. Think of these practices as turns on a mountain.

The question that is the through-line for this book is: **What will we do differently to create a better place to work?**

To get started, pick one, two or three practices that you want to try, and be open to the possibilities of what will emerge from developing these new habits. When you get there, what are the next three? If you miss one, you'll need to course-correct along the way. We must trust the emergent process because we're not going to know the next turns until we embark on the first ones.

Shifting culture is about what we practice. I can begin a practice today and start applying it in my workplace tomorrow. I can introduce it to my team—one practice, one person at a time. I can impact change, and that's powerful.

A Better Way

There is a new vision of work emerging. It is about flourishing versus surviving. It is possible to achieve what everyone wants—an opportunity to contribute. It is possible to create great, high-quality work in your organization and to reap the benefits. And it often means going against the grain of the direction that work is taking in this society. It means being positively deviant and developing workplace practices that transform the psychological and emotional environment!

To me, there is hope in knowing that positive culture shifts happen through the practices of individual people and teams. It makes it personal. We can choose to practice exhaustion, mindlessness and lack of integrity, or we can choose to practice resilience, mindfulness and transformational leadership.

What story are you choosing?

ACTIVITIES

Personal Practices:

1. Think about the best workplace or work team you have ever experienced. Write down as many words as you can to describe this workplace or team.

   _____

   _____

   Now think about your worst workplace experience. Write down as many words as you can to describe this workplace or team.

   _____

   _____

   Compare the lists. What do these words describe? Chances are that the words you used describe the culture. Usually when

I ask people this question they use words like respect, trust, positive, communication, caring, openness and collaborative to describe their best workplace. When they describe their worst workplace, they use words like blame, bullying, top-down, unfair, disrespected, negative or undervalued. What words did you use?

I do this exercise to show people that what makes a workplace great or not-so-great is the culture. And yet, when organizations set out to create a better, healthier workplace they typically do not focus on culture. Try this exercise at your next team meeting to stimulate discussion.

2. There is a practice called "focused writing" that is used to help you explore a topic and come up with new, creative solutions. There is something about the act of writing that unlocks a different part of our brain than we use when simply thinking or talking about the issue.

Get a blank note pad or journal and set a timer for 5 minutes. Consider the question *"what will be different tomorrow if there is a positive shift in my workplace today?"* and begin writing. The idea with focused writing is that you do not take your pen off the paper and instead keep writing whatever comes to mind. If you can't think of anything to say, write "I can't think of anything to say." Eventually the words will start to flow. Don't worry about clarity or spelling, no one will see this but you. Just write until the timer goes. Try this creative process and see if it helps you to come up with new solutions or sort through different ideas in your mind.

Take another five minutes and do focused writing using the question *"what is my through-line?"* Let the ideas flow and just write until the timer goes off. Then go back and circle anything that stands out for you.

3. Begin a one-page personal leadership plan which includes your through-line goals (What do I want our culture to be?). You can include the practices you will start with, or you can add these in as you read the book. I developed this way of planning by following some of the ideas in Hugh Culver's book "Give Me a Break."[10] Divide your page as follows:

Through-line Culture Goals (these are your overarching goals)

e.g.

- Improve positivity in my team this year so that we are working cohesively, creatively and productively.

My goals are: _____

_____

_____

Plan for This Week (these are your first three turns)

e.g.

- Focused writing on 'What do I want our culture to be?"
- Observe what our current challenges are and where we need practices to shift these
- Examine my hypocrisies as a leader

My goals are: _____

_____

_____

Plan for this Month (these are practices or tasks you want to develop this month but are not your first three turns)

e.g

- Read through this entire book and look at other leadership, team and organizational practices that can be implemented
- Do the best/worst workplace exercise with my team
- Start a gratitude journal and just observe what it does for me

My plan this month is: _____

_____

_____

Someday Plans (ideas you don't want to lose sight of, but are not in your short-term plan)

e.g

- Consider a culture survey for our team/organization
- Consider offering some instruction on mindfulness/meditation and developing a meditation/quiet room for employees to use throughout the day

My someday plans include: _____

_____

_____

Each week, check in with your vision. What is on your through-line for this week? Evaluate. If what you're doing is not feeding your through-line, then what course-correction is needed? What are your next three turns? What is on the plan for this month and on your someday list? What can you add to this plan as you move through the rest of the book?

Team Practice:

Discuss this chapter with your team. Together, discuss your vision for a better place to work and pick your first three turns. What are the first three practices that will best move you toward your goal? Work through, develop and tailor these practices, one by one, as you learn about them throughout this book. Change course when needed.

The first three turns that will best move my team toward our vision are:

1. _____

2. _____

3. _____

Organizational Practice:

Examine the "costs of doing nothing" in your organization. What are the negative outcomes you are seeing that are related to not addressing your culture? Examples include turnover, absenteeism, presenteeism, lack of innovation, productivity, customer service, overwhelmed and underutilized employees, benefit costs, costs of short- and long-term disability, EAP costs, and more. What other costs might there be?

Featured Influencer: Dr. Martin Shain

Martin Shain S.J.D.

Dr. Martin Shain is principal and founder of the Neighbour at Work Centre, a consulting agency in workplace mental health established in 2004, and a lecturer in the School of Public Health at the University of Toronto.

Drawing on his background in law and social science, Martin consults with workplace stakeholders to help them understand and address their current and emerging responsibilities in order to provide and maintain psychologically safe and healthy workplaces.

Martin wrote three policy discussion papers for the Mental Health Commission of Canada that provide key foundations for, and a prototype of, the National Standard on Psychological Health and Safety in the Workplace issued in 2013.

He is an ongoing core member of the multipartite Technical Committee that developed the National Standard into its present form.

Martin helped develop the criteria for Canada's Safest Employers Psychological Safety Award and subsequently served as a judge to review applications for the first two years of its existence.

His most recent book is "The Careful Workplace: seeking psychological safety at work in the era of Canada's national standard," published by Thomson Reuters in 2016.

Dr. Shain was the recipient of the Canadian Workplace Wellness Pioneer Award.

More about Dr. Shain's work and publications can be found at www.neighbouratwork.com.

CHAPTER 2

Engage in Practices

"Leadership is action, not a position. Leaders who inspire, foster creativity; who mentor, build confidence; who listen, build respect; who model desired behaviours, receive the same in return. Leadership is not a title; it is about impact, influence and inspiration. Healthy cultures invite everyone to be a leader."
—Anonymous participant in the Positive Workplace Culture Thoughtexchange 2015

What do we want our culture to be? This simple question was the starting point for a bold new vision for Baptist Healthcare (BHC), an organization that led the way in creating a workplace where wellness was possible. They reaped the benefits as a result—higher employee satisfaction, lower turnover, greater patient satisfaction and lower patient mortality.[11] All this has landed BHC in the top 25 on Fortune's "100 Best Places to Work" in America, every year now since 2002.

What is unique about BHC's story is that they didn't take a "boxed" approach to creating a healthy culture. Instead they asked, "what will make our employees happy?"

We brought in Al Stubblefield, who was the president of BHC at the time, to keynote at the Conference in 2006. He shared with us the journey they made to create a positive culture, saying that "culture will drive strategy, or culture will drag strategy." Here is the story of BHC, summarized from Stubblefield's keynote and book.

Back in the 1990's, when most workplace health initiatives were taking a disease-prevention approach, BHC started doing things differently. The impetus for change was the fact that they were experiencing a slow downward spiral.

According to Stubblefield, the decline was due to many factors, including merger discussions, poor management decisions, and an attempt at re-engineering. They had lost focus and vision. The issues this presented included patient satisfaction scores at the 18th percentile (this means that 82% of the competing hospitals surveyed had higher patient satisfaction), employee satisfaction scores that were well below the norm, very high employee turnover, and patient mortality being one of the highest amongst their competitors.

Their decision to make quality their focus was at first only an attempt to survive. But as they went down this path of evaluating their current state and doing research, they made the link between unhappy employees and unhappy customers. Looking at their data, they realized that they were asking their employees to help people get well in an employee culture that was unwell.

They recognized the need to increase employee happiness to get the highest performance from their staff. We hear a lot about happiness and positivity in the workplace these days, but back in the nineties this thinking was unique.

Here are a few of the numerous practices BHC implemented.

Creating a Bold Vision

BHC knew they needed a vision that would tap into the passion people had for the work they did in healthcare. Following advice from Jim Collins and Jerry Porras's best-selling book "Built to Last: Successful Habits of Visionary Companies,"[12] they made their vision a BHAG (Big Hairy Audacious Goal): "Our vision is to be the best health system in America."

This vision was developed after two days of brainstorming with all of the senior leaders, followed by four months of sitting with it and asking questions throughout the organization.

Practicing Positive Deviance

At a time when management was more top-down and hierarchical than it is now, BHC was deviating from the norm in a positive way. They were determined that their people would always come first. This also meant that leadership had to change, and for many this was a painful adjustment.

Asking Transformational Questions

Every employee at BHC had the opportunity to have input into questions that helped form the mission, vision, values and new culture, such as:

• What do we want our culture to be?
• Why do we exist? (mission)
• What are we striving to become? (vision)
• What guides our everyday behaviour? (values)

These are great questions for any organization to ask when embarking on this path. Stubblefield also suggests that senior managers ask themselves these questions:

• What do your employees think that you think is important?
• How do they know? (As a senior leader, are you talking about what is important to you? Are you leading by example?)

Engaging Employees in the Change

BHC tapped into their employees' passion through continual conversation and gave them a reason to want to change. They asked employees what originally brought them to the work that they do, and what could make it better. They offered the opportunity to discover and define the new culture, and they rewarded the behaviours that they wanted to see. A new WOW! Workplace was developed, which stands for "Empowering our **Workers** to become **Owners** and **Winners**."

This was a radical cultural transformation, which included systematically replacing negative aspects of the culture with positive practices that served the new environment. The leaders at BHC understood that people generally want to be the best they can be, and they set out to develop a culture that allowed them to achieve it. The result was that within nine months their patient satisfaction scores reached the 75th percentile. Eighteen months after starting, employees rated BHC above the norm in 17 out of 18 measures (prior, this had only been five).

Two years later, the consultants who conducted the survey had never seen such high results. By 2002, patient satisfaction scores were in the 99th percentile, employee turnover was cut in half, mortality rates were down, and they were #10 on America's 100 Best Companies to Work For listing in Fortune Magazine, determined by the Great Place to Work® Institute. What really makes this a great story, however, is that the changes they've made were long-lasting and sustainable, and the company still reaps the benefits to this day.

Our Conference Team in 2006 was so impressed with what BHC had done that we incorporated some of their ideas into the way we ran our organization. One idea we implemented was a "Service Recovery Budget." This was a simple concept of adding $250 to our annual Conference budget, which was available to any staff member to use at any time to recover from a service mistake. For example, if a conference delegate or sponsor was unhappy in any way, the Conference team knew they could tap into that budget to buy a coffee, pay for a cab fare, or do whatever it took to make the situation right.

In all the years that we had that Service Recovery line in our budget, I think we only used it once. However, the benefit of having it there was that it gave our team the ownership to do the right thing. It was empowering.

Another one of these ideas was giving out WOW! certificates. We picked one person on our team each month who had gone above and beyond in some way and made them a certificate that told them how outstanding they were and what we appreciated about them, and then we all signed it. I still have one on my office wall that the team made for me. It thanks me for helping them strive to live a balanced life. It reminds me of a great team who took ownership in making our work together fun and meaningful, and who took to heart the lessons we were learning from the various thought-leaders who came to share their stories with us.

> What leadership practices will you adopt to create a positive people culture?

What is a Positive Culture?

Much of the research on workplace wellness analyzes programs, but the data shows that organizational and personal well-being does not change dramatically with this method. Focusing our efforts on making the culture more positive is far more likely to be effective. Dr. Michael West is Europe's leading expert on healthcare leadership and its impact on financial sustainability. He and his associates have reviewed the literature on climate and culture over the past 50 years. Their finding is that the most significant influence we can have on the culture is through leadership. As Dr. West has said, "If we can get to a situation where leaders are behaving in compassionate ways (the four behaviours being attending, understanding, empathizing and supporting), this is what begins to transform cultures. It is vital."

In the Thoughtexchange, the organizational health community was asked the question, "what is a positive workplace?" The majority said that a positive workplace was characterized by supportive leadership as well as leaders who walk the talk and who make themselves available and open to their staff. Other comments that rose to the top of this online discussion were:

"Good management is health promotion. Having management with excellent people skills and treating people with fairness and respect is essential to a positive work culture. If you have your employees' best interests at heart, they will follow you anywhere."

"A positive workplace is characterized by leaders that 'block and tackle' so you can do your job. It enables the employee to focus on what is really important for their job to get it done."

Respondents discussed how recognizing others' contributions and feeling that you are making a contribution and are valued is important to a positive workplace. They talked about how important it is that all team members' contributions are acknowledged.

It was stated that in a positive culture, there are practices in place that establish expectations around how team members will contribute and what they can expect in return. Here are some of the individual comments that received a lot of stars:

"We do not know what another person has on their plate

today! We need to acknowledge that we are all human and that we each face our own set of unique circumstances every day. Showing respect for each other personally, professionally and socially will help us to build community. It builds strong teams with common goals."

"A positive workplace is a place where people feel respected and valued for the work they do. This needs to be more than formal words in mission statements, but demonstrated by the way people are treated by all management and supervisory staff."

Another characteristic of a positive culture that came up was recognition. It was noted that when employees feel appreciated, they are more likely to go above and beyond what is expected of them. Suggestions made for recognition included learning how your employees like to be rewarded (a thank you versus a gift, time off versus a certificate, etc.) and being consistent with rewards.

A common thread that came out of the discussion was the need to create a culture of appreciation, trust, respect, positivity, health and wellness.

Expert Interviews

Each of the thought-leaders interviewed for this book were also asked the question "what is a positive workplace?" Their individual responses are captured below. Consider what they say, and perhaps there is a description here or a combination of words from what each had to say that resonates with you and can be tailored to use in your workplace as you go forward.

From Robert Quinn: "A positive organization is a system in which the people flourish and exceed expectations."

From Linda Duxbury: "People want to come to work. There is mutual respect. People feel safe enough to speak up if they see something wrong, or if someone is behaving inappropriately, and know they will not be punished."

From Michael West: "A positive work culture is one where people have a sense of being involved in an enterprise that is making a positive difference and is something that they can be proud of. It's one where people are clear about what it is they are required to do, and they get clear feedback about how well they are performing which enables them to improve and to feel confident.

"It's a culture where people are respected and valued and cared for, and where there's a sense of mutual compassion. It is a positive people culture—so that people experience positive emotions, optimism, cohesion, gratitude, humour, and consequently, a sense of engagement.

"It's a culture where there is a commitment to learning and innovation, to finding new and improved ways of doing things, where people are given the space, support, resources and training to innovate.

"It's a culture where there are well-developed teams. The teams work effectively in themselves, where there's good inter-team working for the overall cause of the organization. It's a culture where leadership is collective, rather than predominantly hierarchical. Where everyone feels they can take shared responsibility, there is shared leadership and teams, and where leaders work interdependently together."

From Graham Lowe: "A healthy organization is at once healthy, successful and responsible. I incorporate in a healthy organization model three previously separate streams of management practice and research: workplace health promotion, organizational performance, and social responsibility.

"It is people-focused values that are meaningful and that guide workplace interactions and people's behaviour in their jobs, and they can take different forms. In health care, you'll see 'caring' as a value, but in manufacturing you'll see words reflecting a supportive workplace. The words need to resonate with those who are in the organization. They need to make sense to the nature of the business and they need to be alive. They need to be guideposts for people's interactions; not only how they interact with each other, but also how they go about doing their jobs."

From Mary Ann Baynton: "A positive workplace culture is one where we can have different opinions and different perspectives and respectfully discuss them. It is a place where we have a way to resolve conflicts effectively, and people are not afraid to speak up or disagree."

From Melissa Barton: "A positive workplace is one where people reflect. One of the things we really focus on is 'increasing reflective capacity.' At the end of each day, people stop and reflect—how did that go? How did I feel about that conversation? How do I think the other person felt in that conversation? How could I do better? We're trying to do a lot of reflective work so that people respond rather than react."

From Mary-Lou MacDonald: "A positive culture is a place where individually and collectively we are supported in reaching our potential. We have collective goals and individual goals. By supporting individuals to reach their full potential intellectually, psychologically, physically, spiritually and emotionally, the organization reaches its potential as well."

From Gregor Breucker: "The psychological qualities of adults are key to a positive culture. The existing qualities in working life are the result of early experiences in family life, a basis which is not easily open to changes in later stages of life. I also do believe that a fundamental pre-requisite in any society is a much more balanced approach to organizing access to wealth and economically-based life chances.

"Most societies in the industrialized world have produced too many people and families who are objectively underprivileged and cannot escape precarious living conditions. Politically this is severely threatening all democratic societies in the Western world, resulting in increased violence, criminality, and even fascist tendencies in many societies.

"Working life cannot develop positive cultures without a solution to the social question and without ensuring a sufficient level of social cohesion. This also applies to a culture development within organizations.

"This perspective is certainly a European and a German one and very much influenced by the specific model of capitalism which was developed historically in my country [Germany] after the war and which still is the motor of economic prosperity."

From Marie Mac Donald: "A positive workplace culture is a culture where people show up and do their best work and there is psychological safety as a minimum. Ideally, there is a culture of innovation, creativity, trust, respect, authenticity and integrity, and always a strong focus, care and concern about people's health and wellness."

From Martin Shain: "I'm coming from the perspective of mental health and thinking about this through the lens of the new National Standard on Psychological Health & Safety in the Workplace. Within that Standard there are three main elements: 1) governance philosophy, 2) psychological health & safety management system (usually considered the backbone of the Standard), and 3) a cultural design piece.

"The cultural design piece is intimated in the Standard but never really spelled out. What it means to me is what is known as 'culture by design as opposed to by default.' Cultural design is a deliberately promoted set of integrated values, beliefs, attitudes and practices based on the requirements of a 'Careful Workplace' (one that conserves individual, social and economic capital by causing no foreseeable physical or psychological harm to individuals) and promulgated through recruitment, hiring, promotion, orientation, training, and workplace practices. To have a positive workplace culture, then, requires the avoidance of foreseeable harm.

"Surprisingly, even the most sophisticated organizations often miss the boat on these key principles.

"I want to see these principles embedded in the way things are done and how people are managed, rather than offering a new program. It's not a program. It's a process that has to be intimated into the way of doing business."

Moving from Programs to Practices

In the Thoughtexchange, the community was asked, "What practices have you experienced (or heard of) that have improved workplace culture?" Here are 14 great ideas for practices that were suggested. Which of these practices can you tailor to use in your workplace?

- **Team Huddles:** Short, daily stand-up meetings—just to check in on workload, how everyone is doing, and who needs help.
- **Positive Reinforcement:** Performance management systems that reward positive behaviour.
- **Recognition Programs:** Give staff the opportunity to submit nominations for others. Use current workplace award systems that are available in your workplace or create your own. Recipients feel good knowing that others think highly

of them, and it makes those submitting nominations look for positive aspects within their work life. All in all, this promotes positive thoughts and interactions.

- **Recognition Toolkit:** A Not-For-Profit organization I am involved with gave every leader an actual "recognition toolkit" with recognition resources. Keep it simple.
- **Clear Roles:** Establish explicit expectations around contributions and what the team member can reasonably receive in exchange.
- **Brainstorming:** In an organization I worked with, we had brainstorming sessions regularly. It didn't matter what we brainstormed, just that we got together and did it. Sometimes it was directly work-related and sometimes it was discussing the potluck or a work anniversary.
- **Positive Story to Start Your Meeting:** This sets the tone and culture. Very simple and costs nothing!
- **Use Positive Measures:** Don't just focus on lagging and negative measures like absenteeism and the number of employee relations cases. Measure healthy workplace practices like "How often are recognition systems being used?" "How many high potential performers have you identified?" Remember the adage "what gets measured gets time and attention."
- **Invest in Your Culture:** Creating a positive culture requires sustained commitment and an investment of time and money. Things that are important to invest in include training and development, supports like coaching and mentoring, opportunities for face-to-face interaction, recognition programs, and measuring progress.
- **Educate Management About High-Stress Cultures:** Provide education for top management on the financial consequences of a high-stress culture (busyness, multi-tasking, due yesterday, never enough). Help management become more realistic in

their expectations and realize that it is workers' performance and productivity that make up the organization.

- **Outside Experts:** Bring in experts once in a while to lead a workshop on workplace health. It's often helpful to have someone who is not part of the team but who is an expert highlight avenues and goals for us to improve cohesiveness, collaboration, and respect.

- **Demonstrate the Culture:** Leaders who model the culture they want have a powerful influence on staff. This is done by consistently demonstrating the behaviours and actions that characterize the culture you want, continuously expressing your vision, and recognizing those who exemplify the culture you want.

- **Improved Emotional Intelligence:** We all have varying degrees of emotional intelligence—the ability to recognize and handle both our own emotions and those of others. This skill set can be learned and the degree to which it is applied in the workplace has a direct effect on culture.

- **Identify Where Support is Needed:** Identify areas that are under pressure and ensure there is support. This goes a long way toward employees feeling valued, and will in turn make them ambassadors of the organization.

Practices in Action

I asked Dr. Graham Lowe for an example of when positive practices had successfully created a positive culture shift. Dr. Lowe is currently the president of the workplace consulting firm The Graham Lowe Group Inc. and was a keynote speaker at the Conference on a few occasions. He told me a story about the Alberta School Employee Benefits Plan (ASEBP), who he worked with in 1998 and then again in 2016. ASEBP is a not-for-profit organization that provides benefits to the people who work in the public education system from Kindergarten to Grade 12 in Alberta.

Back in 1998, Edmonton Public Schools were very committed to improving the health of their workplace. They set up a "Healthy Organization" committee to create a more health-promoting work environment and to identify those groups who needed the most help. Dr. Lowe was a professor at the University of Alberta at the time and was hired to do data integration and analysis. He quoted:

In 1998, there was a partnership between ASEBP and Edmonton Public Schools. They were looking at organizational health, so we analyzed the claims data (absenteeism, etc.) and mapped this with workforce demographics to see which groups were at high risk and needing help. That was a very early example of the kind of research that connects the dots—they had a union-management wellness committee. It was quite ahead of its time then.

Dr. Lowe went on to tell me about the small steps this organization has taken each year, expanding the supports it offers to the 55,000 people that it provides plans for. He just completed a project with them which looked at resilience in leadership. This involved surveys and consultations with educational leaders, first linking the research on positive organizational studies and positive psychology to leadership capabilities and then connecting that to well-being.

They used it with leaders, asking "what can we learn from this to enhance our programs to support people, especially around mental well-being and job performance?" From Dr. Lowe:

Watching them, they have been through a succession of leaders, but the common glue is a very strong internal culture that gives the highest priority to individuals' well-being—both employees and clients. They are incredibly supportive of each other. They communicate well. They model this. They're always looking at how they can enhance well-being. I found it very interesting to go back after 18 years and see what they had been doing.

Lowe indicated that they used the measure of psychological capital to link positive psychology to well-being. Psychological capital has four components which are resilience, hope, optimism and efficacy (the feeling that you can do something to improve your situation). He found that people who were high on those measures reported better well-being, both mentally and physically, and showed more indication of a transformational leadership style. Now, when they are communicating internally, they can say that better well-being actually makes you a better leader.

Often it seems that projects like these can't get off the ground. Despite our best efforts, sometimes the organization is not prepared to take the necessary steps. Numerous respondents in the Thoughtexchange stated the need to create change from within "even if my organization is not ready."

In my interview with Dr. Michael West, Professor of Organizational Psychology at the Lancaster University Management School, I asked for his recommendation on shifting culture from within, and if change must start at the top.

I don't think it has to start at the top. It's much easier if it does. But my recommendation is don't try to do it by yourself. The defense mechanisms in organizations are likely to ensure that you are chewed up and spat out.

There is a fascinating area of social psychology called minority influence theory. It is based on work about how minorities will bring about change in communities.

We always focus on how majorities get people to conform and fit in, but this is about how minorities can bring about change, and what it suggests is that you need to form a small group of committed people who share your vision. And then to articulate a small number of clear messages about the kind of culture you want to achieve and the changes that you want to make. And then to have a strategy where you repeat and repeat those messages in any forum or through any media that you can, so the cohesive and clear small group is taking responsibility to evangelize about those key messages.

Be sure to listen carefully to what people's responses are, but commit to repeating and repeating messages. And over time, what the evidence shows, is it causes people to think more creatively about the issues. They don't just go along with what the "majority view" is but begin to think creatively around the issues, and that frees up thinking.

You can take the examples of these groups that existed in the seventies and eighties—like the greens and the feminists—and they have changed the way that we think because they had a vision and they were cohesive. And they talked about these consistent messages coherently, repeatedly, and bravely. I think that is a powerful strategy for bringing about change. It is clear that people who try as individuals to bring about change and don't form such a small group on the whole either get exhausted or spat out by the organization.

Dr. West advised that the small group must model the behaviours they want others to incorporate. He believes that if we want to bring about profound change, we need to practice compassion and listening with fascination to others in order to understand their situation and empathize.

As a leader, this means asking the question: **"How can I help you?"**

ACTIVITIES

Personal Practices:

1. Dr. Robert Quinn shares an exercise in his book "Building the Bridge As You Walk On It: A Guide for Leading Change" that involves the use of appreciative inquiry as a tool. His premise is that if you want to transform your organization, you must first transform yourself. It's often easy to identify our flaws, or even areas where we excel, but it is harder to get to our unique skills—the ways that we most create value for the world. When we uncover these skills and spend more time doing the things that only we can do, we create more value and positive change for our organizations.

   The exercise is to contact 15-25 people who know you best (such as work colleagues, friends, and family) and ask them to help identify your unique value. I found using an email was the easiest way to do this. Ask the question "when I am at my best, who am I?"

   Below is an example of the email I sent to my contacts when doing this exercise. Use whatever feels useful to you from this example, or create your own. Gather whatever comments come in and look for where they overlap. Notice what this feedback does for you.

   Dear Friends & Colleagues,

   As a part of a leadership program I have embarked on I am contacting you for some feedback. I'm getting in touch with you because you know me well, either as a work-colleague or as a friend, or both. My assignment is to identify the unique skills I have that create the most value for others.

   The question I am asking is this: "when I am at my very best, what are the unique positive characteristics that I have?"

   If you could take a moment to reflect on this question and send

*me some brief feedback I would be most grateful! It can be a story, an
example or as simple as a word or two. Anything you send is much
appreciated!*

When I did this exercise, I received many responses that surprised
me. What do you think this made me want to do? It made me want to
be at my best all the time!

Try extending this to your team by having each team member
reflect and then write about "Who are WE when we're at our best?"
Facilitate a meeting where you capture and record what people say.
Post the results. Observe what this does for your team.

2. This exercise is adapted from Rosamund and Ben Zander's book "The
    Art of Possibility: Transforming Professional and Personal Life."[13]
    Rosamund spoke on this book at the Conference in 2006. They
    suggest that conflict and struggle will often shift to a more enjoyable
    experience with a practice of asking "how will I be a contribution
    today?" Declare yourself to be someone who makes a difference to
    others. Ask this transformational question daily.

    Once in this mindset each day, try also asking the question
    suggested by Michael West: "how can I help you?" We don't always
    need to be the "expert." Ask this question with humility to your team
    or work group and observe what happens.

3. As suggested by Dr. West, rather than trying to be the lone change
    agent, form a small group of like-minded individuals who share your
    vision. Review the suggested practices in this chapter with your group
    and decide on some simple messages and questions to communicate.
    What leadership practices will you adopt personally to create a positive
    people culture? Add these practices to your personal leadership plan.

Team Practice:

Review the suggested practices that came from the Thoughtexchange on improving workplace culture, such as team huddles or starting your meetings with positive stories. Which practices can you tailor to use with your teams?

_____

_____

_____

Organizational Practice:

Start asking this question throughout your organization: "What do we want our culture to be?" Find forums and opportunities to start a discussion on your new vision.

Featured Influencer: Dr. Graham Lowe

Graham Lowe

Graham Lowe's reputation as an expert on work and organizations is based on his successful academic career. Graham has over 30 years of organizational, labour market, and policy consulting experience across Canada and internationally. He is president of The Graham Lowe Group Inc., a workplace consulting and research firm. He also was a founding partner (2005–08) of the Great Place to Work® Institute Canada, an affiliate of the U.S.-based global consulting firm specializing in cultural transformation. He is professor emeritus at the University of Alberta and has been a visiting professor, lecturer, and researcher at other universities in Canada, Europe, and Asia.

Graham is the author of several books, including "Creating Healthy Organizations: How Vibrant Workplaces Inspire Employees to Achieve Sustainable Success." His latest book with Frank Graves is entitled "Redesigning Work: A Blueprint for Canada's Future Well-Being and Prosperity." Graham has given hundreds of conference talks and workshops, across Canada and internationally. He is a recipient of the Canadian Workplace Wellness Pioneer Award and holds a PhD in Sociology from the University of Toronto.

Graham has contributed many articles to practitioner publications, including *Policy Options, Canadian HR Reporter, HR Professional, Health & Productivity Management, Canadian Business, Healthcare Quarterly, Healthcare Papers* and *Qmentum Quarterly.*

Read more about Dr. Lowe's publications and work at www.grahamlowe.ca.

CHAPTER 3

POSITIVELY DEVIANT

"There are people in your company or group who are already doing things in a radically better way. To create lasting change, find areas of positive deviance and fan their flames."
—**Pascale and Sternin, Harvard Business Review, 2010.**

I once started a new position as a manager with a team who were stuck on doing things a certain way. Being new, I had a lot of questions about why things were done in these ways. My new team would typically answer with comments like "because we've *always* done it that way!" Or if I'd suggest something new, the answer was "that won't work because…" This kind of communication shuts down innovation.

I decided we had to change our approach. Together, we spent time talking about how we could improve our communication, shift our focus to a more transformational approach, and most of all, catch ourselves before answering a question in a way that shut down new ideas. We set some ground rules for our team meetings, and over time this team became more positive and effective. Looking back twenty years on that experience, it was one of the most enjoyable groups I've been involved with. A few years later, this was the small team who ended up starting the first ever Health Work & Wellness™ Conference in Canada!

I consider this change in approach to be an act of positive deviance. Positive deviance is simply behaviour that differs from the norm in honourable ways or for positive reasons. It is deviant because it is "off the beaten path"; it is intentional behaviour that is performed with a positive purpose in mind.[14,15] We did not have this term back in the nineties when I was working with this team, but essentially what we were doing was positively disrupting the normal behaviour of that time.

Being positively deviant in your organization takes courage and requires vision. It is often difficult to go against the grain yourself, let alone bring others with you, but it is necessary for positive change to happen. It means asking questions versus problem solving, and being prepared to go through deep change to find your purpose and vision. It means speaking truth to those in power, and always looking for the proactive stance versus the reactive one.

> How can you be positively deviant today?

The background research and interviews I conducted for this book suggest three shifts in thinking that can help us to positively deviate from the conventional way we do things in the workplace:

1. Shifting from downstream to upstream thinking
2. Shifting from a program approach to a cultural approach
3. Shifting from conventional management to transformational leadership

Let's explore what these three shifts in thinking are.

Shifting from Downstream to Upstream Thinking

Dr. Donald B Ardell was a keynote at our very first conference in 1997. He wrote a "fable" in his first book, "High Level Wellness: An

Alternative to Doctors, Drugs and Disease"[16] to make a point about the need to focus on prevention. As he said, Merriam-Webster defines a fable as a "fictitious narrative or statement, a legendary story of supernatural happenings or a narration intended to enforce a useful truth." With his permission, I have modified this fable to focus on the workplace:

It was many years ago that villagers in Downstream recall spotting the first body in the river. Some old timers remember how sparse the facilities and procedures were back then for managing that sort of thing. Sometimes, they say, it would take hours to pull ten people from the river, and even then only a few would survive.

Though the number of victims in the river has increased greatly in recent years, the good folks of Downstream have responded admirably to the challenge. Their rescue system is clearly second to none; most people discovered in the swirling waters are reached within twenty minutes, many in less than ten. Only a small number drown each day before help arrives—a big improvement from the way it used to be.

Talk to the people of Downstream and they'll speak with pride about the new treatment centre by the edge of the waters, the flotilla of rescue boats ready for service at a moment's notice, and the comprehensive plan for handling these victims until they can get back to work—disability management, employee assistance counseling services and even an absenteeism management program!

There are many highly trained and dedicated swimmers always ready to risk their lives to save victims from the raging currents, and full-time return-to-work coordinators to help get them back to work when they're ready. Sure, it costs a lot but, say the Downstreamers, "what else can decent people do except to provide whatever is necessary when human lives are at stake?"

Oh, a few people in Downstream have raised the question,

"What is happening Upstream?" *now and again, but most folks show little interest. It seems there's so much to do to help those in the river that nobody's got time to check how all those bodies are getting there in the first place. That's the way things are sometimes.*

As one of my favourite authors, Patti Digh, says, "You can be busy, or you can be remarkable." Sometimes when we're stuck in downstream, we can get so busy managing crises that we forget, or we're too tired or busy, to look upstream to see why they are happening.

Many organizations focus their attention downstream, primarily on the 10% of employees who cost them the most in disability and sick leave. I believe this is the wrong approach. This tactic runs the risk of neglecting the other 90%—those creative, talented, productive individuals that we work so hard to recruit. This is in part what Stubblefield said happened with BHC before their transformation. They took their eye off the ball, and hadn't noticed what was going on upstream with their employees.

Canada has had a big role to play in taking the upstream approach, starting with "A New Perspective on the Health of Canadians" (the Lalonde Report) originally released in 1974, which was considered to have led to the development of the idea of health promotion.[17]

The Ottawa Charter for Health Promotion was developed in 1986 at the first International Conference on Health Promotion. In this document, health promotion was defined as such:

Health promotion is the process of enabling people to increase control over, and to improve, their health. To reach a state of complete physical, mental and social well-being, an individual or group must be able to identify and to realize aspirations, to satisfy needs, and to change or cope with the environment. Health is, therefore, seen as a resource for everyday life, not the objective of living. Health is a positive concept emphasizing social and personal resources, as well as physical capacities. Therefore, health promotion is not just the responsibility of the health sector, but goes beyond healthy life-styles to well-being.[18]

What happened to this perspective over the years, and how did we come to the place in our workplaces where health promotion efforts focus mostly on reducing disease symptoms? Diagram 3 outlines many of the services offered in workplaces today, which are primarily downstream and focused on disease-prevention versus wellness.

DIAGRAM #3 Most Organizational Health Efforts are Downstream Focused

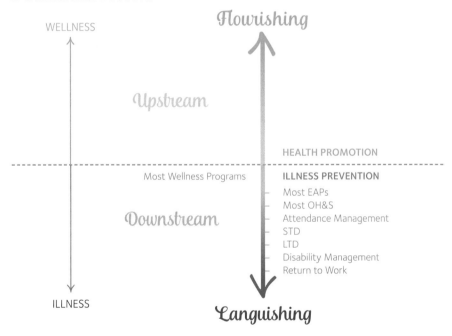

Thinking about what your organization offers related to the health of its employees, is it more upstream or downstream-focused? Multidisciplinary literature indicates that organizational health can only be achieved by focusing on the organization as a system, and yet the approach taken by most organizations is usually more superficial.[19] As the 2013 Sanofi Canada Healthcare Survey notes, "Organizations need to look at what they have within their control to start creating a wellness culture, which is the foundation and underpinning of anything that an individual can or should do. It's within every organization's power to take these steps, whether you're big, small, union or non-union."[20]

If we are to build wellness into our workplaces, we need to get clear on what that means. This term was first coined by Dr. Halbert L. Dunn in a book called "High Level Wellness" in 1961.[21] He defined it as "[a]n integrated method of functioning which is oriented toward maximizing the potential of which the individual is capable, within the environment where he is functioning." The National Wellness Institute in the US further defined it as "an active process through which people become aware of, and make choices toward, a more successful existence."[22]

As Quinn says, when you focus on a problem (downstream), all that is available to you are the fixes to that problem. You're not seeing the whole picture, and you miss the possibilities. By focusing on the vision instead (e.g. a workplace where people have continual renewal, can be creative, and feel valued) and then developing practices that will achieve that vision, you will come to different solutions. What are you doing upstream in your organization to create a culture of psychological and emotional well-being?

Practices in Action

Dr. Michael West provided an example of starting a business with these goals in mind and how much easier it is to manage that way. He ran a business school called Aston Business School for four years, and the team he worked with put the principles from all their research into practice. For example, they made sure there was a clear vision for the organization; that there were understandable, challenging and agreed-upon objectives that were established in the appraisals; and that the performance appraisals were good conversations. They created a positive climate with lots of appreciation, gratitude, support and reward for innovation. They focused on good team-work as well as good communication between different teams. From Dr. West:

> *What was remarkable was how extraordinarily well the organization functioned. It achieved a 50% growth in revenue, the morale of the staff was sky-high, it was the best of any academic institution in Britain, and student satisfaction was very high. But also, what was really striking for me was that it is so much easier to manage that way than any other way. It's just a joy.*
>
> *Of course, you must deal with those people who behave aggressively, inappropriately, or who are just not trying to perform—that small, tiny percentage of individuals. But if we manage organizations by focusing on those sorts of behaviours then we're lost. We must focus on the positive behaviours, but be prepared to deal with those exceptional cases that come along, in a decisive way. For me that was a profound and joyful learning experience, about putting the principles we're talking about into operation in an organization.*

Shifting from a Program Approach to a Cultural Approach

As Dr. Robert Quinn says in "The Deep Change Field Guide: A Personal Course to Discovering the Leader Within," launching a company-wide change effort without considering the role of culture in the process is the equivalent of "learning that your brain surgeon is ignorant of the organ known as the heart."[23]

A couple of decades ago, I was an employee in an organization going through a massive change process. It appeared to me that not enough thought was put into understanding the culture of the organization and how that would impact the results of this effort. To start with, an expert consultant was brought in from another city, which had a very different culture. While people in our organization came to work in Birkenstocks and casual clothes under their lab coats, the consultant showed up in a power suit, high heels, big hair and big jewelry. There was already a divide before we even began.

This was the umpteenth change effort in the short time I'd been with the company, and the consultant could do little to get people engaged in the process. People felt that this was "the flavour of the month," and that if they could just go with the flow it would soon pass and we'd be on to the next thing. And that is exactly what happened.

If the culture will not support the change, it won't happen. Just as Al Stubblefield said, the culture can drag the proposed strategy down if the effort does not take it into account.

Practices in Action

I interviewed Marie Mac Donald, who has spoken at the Conference numerous times about the cultural approach to healthy organizational change. She is a coach, consultant and speaker with a Master's in Social Work and is a certified Emotional Intelligence (EI) practitioner. She will often get called into a workplace going through change in order to bring the human side into the equation. I asked her how she uses this approach with her clients, and her response was as follows:

> The "what" is the strategy or vision of where you want to go. The "how" is the people and how they are going to get there. I come in with the intention to support their people through change. And then I need to sell them on the fact that you can't engender people's trust and have their engagement in the change if you can't make it psychologically safe for them, and that is what EI is all about.

One of the biggest factors is becoming a learning organization where it's OK to make mistakes. There is an inquiry that takes place when there is a mistake, rather than punishing people while asking them for great innovation.

Marie thinks that doing emotional intelligence work is at the heart of change, and it needs to be ongoing. This allows organizations to move through their challenges and engage their people in the process.

The only way to move through challenges is to have a focus on a healthy workplace at the same time. "Healthy workplace" is not over here to the right, and "transformational change" is over there to the left, and "how you treat your employees" is over here on the back burner. It's looking at the whole system together.

Shifting from Conventional Management to Transformational Leadership

Transformational leadership does all the above. Transformational leaders take an upstream approach and focus on culture. They are positively deviant. Quinn defines transformational leaders as those who can effectively improve culture.[24] They can create deep change by inspiring people to move beyond their own interests to focus on the common good. Here are three practices to help you become a more transformational leader:

Examining Hypocrisy

Self-transformation is critical to transforming organizations. Quinn recommends examining your hypocrisies as a leader as a method of self-transformation. What would happen if we all examined our hypocrisies and then worked at removing them? Sometimes we're so caught up in what we're supposed to be that we fail to see how hypocritical our actions are and how damaging this is, not only for our own health but also to the integrity of our leadership.

Like every leader, I have had my hypocritical moments. Once was in the year of 2001 as I was leading the team heading into the 5ᵗʰ annual Conference—our first ever in Calgary, Alberta.

My problem was that I was coming into this conference exhausted and stressed. We had some growing pains the year prior and had experienced a loss. Although we were heading into this conference with 475 delegates registered and it was a very financially successful year, it had been a tough haul and the cracks were showing.

To add to the stress, my Communications Manager got me a spot on the morning television show the day before the conference. This meant losing a day of preparation time to fly in a day early, staying up late preparing, and then getting up extremely early the next morning to get to the studio. While I would normally appreciate the extra marketing, agreeing to do this show meant adding an extra helping of strain to my pre-conference experience.

Not being a morning person, I could hardly remember my name let alone be an impactful ambassador for wellness. When I think back on it, who would want to attend a wellness conference led by such an exhausted leader? It was a wake-up call for me.

We went on to put on a fantastic event, but there was another red flag the next day. One of the long-time attendees called me over and said, "Deb, you really should hear what this person has to say." He introduced me to a newcomer to the conference. I sat down to speak with her and she went on to say what a great event it was and how much she was learning. But, she also observed that she hadn't seen so many stressed out and tired people in a long time, referring not only to our conference team but also to many of the speakers who were organizational health & wellness professionals, researchers and leadership experts! I had to agree, so I vowed to change this.

What we went on to do after that conference was hold our first-ever one-day retreat as a Conference Team. Not to debrief the event, but to develop our mission and vision going forward, decide how we would work together as a team and how we would schedule and communicate with each other in future, and most importantly determine how we would apply everything we were teaching through this conference to our own team. In other words, we examined our own hypocrisies.

Our mission going forward was *"creating extraordinary workplaces by developing extraordinary people."* The word "extraordinary" was important to us, as we knew that healthy workplaces were not the norm, but were extra-ordinary. With that in mind, we set our vision. We wanted *"to see workplace wellness become commonplace so that 'the extraordinary' becomes 'the expected.'"*

What became even more important to us though, were our values and how we cared for each other. We decided together, as a team, that what we valued was the following:

- **Connection:** connecting people and ideas to create better workplaces by bridging the gap between knowing what to do and doing what should be done.
- **Passion:** we are fueled by our work, the expertise that we share with each other and the passion for creating a better workplace.
- **Generation:** we value growth in people and we support each other through change. We celebrate innovation and the generation of new ideas, encouraging those who choose to find a new or better way.
- **Family:** we are grounded in our two families, our team and the organizational health community across Canada. As a team, we work together like a family, trusting each other, speaking our minds and, most importantly, having fun. With the Canadian

organizational health family, we create opportunities for exchange and discussion while encouraging and empowering everyone to create a better place to work.

The value of "family" was especially important to how we wanted to continue to work together.

We continued to hold a retreat like this annually, and part of our strategy was to bring in an outside facilitator and executive coach. Personally, I also began to pay closer attention to my own practices around sleep, scheduling, breaks, disconnecting, working smarter and being more aware of what was going on for my team members. As we moved in this direction, a couple of years later we won the newly developed Work-Life BC Award of Merit. This was just further validation that we were taking the right path.

Take a minute to reflect. What are your hypocrisies as a leader, and how can you close the gap between what you say and what you do?

Dr. Linda Duxbury, Professor of Management and Strategy at Carleton University, was a keynote at that same Conference in 2001. She spoke at a couple of our later conferences on the ongoing Balancing Work and Family study that she and Chris Higgins conducted across Canada.[25] They have now completed three national studies on work-life balance (1991, 2001 and 2011) where over 70,000 Canadian employees participated.

In our interview, I asked her to comment on what their research showed about the ways in which business owners and managers are hypocritical when it comes to work-life balance. Her first comment was about how emails are sent 24/7, including on weekends, evenings and holidays. She says there is a disconnect between their talk about the importance of balance and the behaviour they are modeling. In addition to this, they are creating an expectation that employees will respond 24/7. As Dr. Duxbury says:

They talk about believing in balance and children, but they punish people who leave early. They punish people who are not willing to be available on weekends and evenings.

Many managers work incredibly long hours. They can't expect the same of their subordinates, and do not recognize that their subordinates are not in the same place and rewarded in the same way.

The email is the biggest hypocrisy. Emails are sent on Sunday for a meeting on Monday due to last minute planning. The idea that people don't have to answer is absolute nonsense, because your boss may say you don't need to respond, but the very act of receiving that email says that you do. The biggest hypocrisy is this whole connected culture—that because we CAN access you 24/7, you SHOULD get accessed 24/7.

Her research also showed that bosses inappropriately expect things from employees that they are not willing to give themselves, such as participating in 360-degree assessments.

Asking Transformational Questions

One form of appreciative inquiry that helps to shift culture is to start asking transformational questions. These questions shift people's thinking in a positive way, inspire them to take on new challenges and are the best way to get people engaged in a vision. BHC used this approach brilliantly at a particularly low point in their history and had great results, as we saw in Chapter Two. I am incorporating transformational questions throughout this book to provide food for thought on each new topic.

Asking transformational questions helps you to understand what employees want and need. Very simply, what is good for employees is generally good for the organization. As Arianna Huffington states, "There is growing evidence that the long-term health of a company's bottom line and the health of its employees are in fact, very much aligned, and when we treat them as separate, we pay a heavy price, both personally and collectively."[26]

Transformational questions help you to gain knowledge that can be incorporated into your change effort, but they are also a way of getting people involved. The question you use will help you create a new, shared vision and will be as unique as your organizational culture is. Just as I suggest for every other practice in this book, take the time to tailor your questions to fit your organization so that they will be truly transformational in nature.

Here are some examples of questions that, if used at the right time and in the right way, can have a profound effect on transforming your team:

- What do we want our culture to be?
- What is the most powerful action we can take right now?
- How can we work with what is available?
- Where are we? Where do we need to go?
- What do we believe in?
- How does this fit with our purpose and vision?

The question used in the activities in Chapter Two (who am I when I am at my best?) can be a transformational question. When I'm working with a group, I will often send this exercise out ahead of time and ask them to try it. When we debrief during the workshop and I ask them about their experience with it, what I most often hear is "the feedback makes me want to be at my best more often." Isn't this exactly the kind of transformation we want of our team members? It's the kind of question that shifts thinking in a positive way and helps people live into the best versions of themselves.

In 2006, to increase discussion at the Conference and to inspire people to think about how they would use new ideas back in their workplaces, our moderator, Francois Lagarde, introduced the questions

"What?" (What was significant here?) and "Now What?" (What am I going to do with this?) after each keynote and workshop, and delegates took time to discuss. These are two great questions to use together after any significant event in the workplace.

Encouraging Reflective Action

Another way of being more transformational is to practice what Quinn calls "reflective action." This means giving team members the necessary space and time to be reflective, which in turn improves decision-making capacity.

Our corporations are often very geared toward action, and we create and reinforce this in our workplace cultures by rewarding those who speak and act quickly. Quinn describes reflective action as a balance between being too reflective (nothing gets done) and too active (mindless behaviour). The challenge is to be both reflective and active, which we can achieve by making time for reflection when we're away from the current task.

For example, have you ever been struggling to come up with an idea for something at your desk, and then when you walk away from it a stroke of inspiration suddenly hits? Taking this contemplation away from the project increases our capacity for mindfulness when we come back to complete the task.

I interviewed Melissa Barton, who is the Director of Organizational Development and Healthy Workplace for Sinai Health System in Ontario. They have been doing some great work in creating an environment that supports psychological and emotional health and wellness. One interesting initiative is their "Poet-in-Residence Program" which helps to get people reflecting on their actions and their practice.

For certain occasions, they will bring in Ronna Bloom, who is a psychotherapist and poet. She does workshops for teams such as one called "Have you seen the patient?" which gets people reflecting on their practice and really seeing the patient—not just coming in and doing what they need to do to get the job done. From Barton:

In her workshops, she'll read a poem, and then she'll give some prompts and she gives people her five rules of writing, which are:
- *Don't think.*
- *Keep your hand moving.*
- *Don't censor yourself.*
- *You're free to write badly.*
- *You don't have to share.*

She'll give a prompt and then you'll go off and write. Inevitably people do share and then it opens conversations.

We get feedback from these workshops that it provides clarity for people. She comes at situations from a sideways approach, which allows what is really lying underneath to emerge. It helps people to get deeper into their practice.

We get a range of people from nursing students to surgeons that come; some people who've been in the profession for years and years, and who are burnt out. It helps them remember why they came to their profession in the first place. It helps to reinvigorate them.

She also does this with intact teams that are struggling. She will craft a poem that is a current state assessment based on feedback from the team about what is not working—and then she works with the team around what their future state could look like. What do we want? They'll co-create their new vision together. They'll write it. She just helps them to pull together their poems.

Barton talked about a session they held on building and sustaining trust in the workplace. Ronna came in to observe and wrote three poems from what she had experienced being in the room. "Those poems blew everyone away by how she could get underneath what everyone was saying," said Barton. "She just really nailed it."

As a leader, there are many ways to encourage and incorporate reflective action. I once introduced this concept to a team, and after we spent some time discussing our current work situation I asked everyone to take a 10-15-minute walk with a pen and notepad in hand. They were instructed to go outside and walk while contemplating their situation, and just write down anything that came to mind. When we reconvened, the ideas were much more diverse than they would have been had we simply stayed put and brainstormed together. How can you incorporate reflective action into how you lead?

Creating an extraordinary workplace means building a culture where every employee can contribute his or her best. This requires a shift of focus from conventional management to transformational leadership, from a program approach to a cultural focus, and from downstream to upstream thinking. It means paying attention to the other ninety percent.

Do you want to be one of the top places to work in Canada (or in your own country)? Do you want your employees to rave about how great it is to work there? Do you want to spend less time recruiting staff because they're already knocking on your door? Try this positively deviant approach to shifting culture.

ACTIVITIES

Personal Practices:

1. Contemplate these questions about becoming a more transformational leader. Set a timer for 10 minutes, and in your journal write your thoughts about each.
   - In what ways do I want to become a more transformational leader?

- How do I see myself leading differently a year from now?
- What steps am I willing to take to shift away from the norm and be positively deviant at work?

2. Examine your hypocrisies as a leader. Make a list of 10 things you do that are hypocritical. Go back and circle three that you are willing to work on changing now.

3. The next time you are faced with an issue or challenge, ask yourself "what is the transformational question I need right now?" Then use that question to move forward. For example, if you're trying to move forward on a big project, you might ask yourself "what is the most potent way I can spend 15 minutes today toward finishing this project?"

Team Practice:

Try introducing reflective action the next time you lead a team meeting. Rather than the typical brainstorming, give everyone a few minutes to reflect individually, perhaps while walking, and make some notes on the issue at hand. Then, come together to debrief and develop your plan of action as a group. See if you have different results with this approach.

Organizational Practice:

Review the organizational health efforts in your workplace and answer these questions:
- Do we take a program approach or a cultural approach?
- Are most efforts aimed downstream or upstream?

- Would I characterize our company as having more conventional management practices or more transformational leadership practices?
- In what ways can these efforts be shifted?

As always, review your personal leadership plan (through-line from Chapter One) and modify with these new ideas.

Featured Influencer: Dr. Linda Duxbury

Linda Duxbury, PhD.

Dr. Linda Duxbury is one of Canada's most reputable experts on work-life balance and employee well-being. With over 200 peer-reviewed publications, Dr. Duxbury's research has remained relevant over the past three decades, addressing changing workplace demographics, human resources, technological advances and generational differences.

Dr. Duxbury has co-led, along with Dr. Christopher Higgins, three major foundational studies that provide comprehensive portrayals and recommendations on work-life balance in Canada. These national studies involved the unprecedented collection of data from 241 of Canada's largest employers (500+), funded by SSHRC, the National Health Research and Development Program, CIHR and Human Resources and Skills Development Canada. Ten resulting refereed monographs have received significant national and international recognition.

Dr. Duxbury also does research on the role overload construct. Her innovational work on the relationship between having too much to do in the time available, employee mental health and the impact of gender on these relationships has helped changed organizational conversations. Her research on role overload has recently expanded and now focuses on the relationship between the use of email, role overload and mental health (and the impact of role overload on police officers' mental health and change readiness). See https://sprott.carleton.ca/profile/linda-duxbury/ for more information on her research.

Dr. Duxbury was a recipient of the Canadian Workplace Wellness Pioneer Award. Her most recent co-authored book "Something's Got to Give: Balancing Work, Childcare and Eldercare" (University of Toronto Press, 2017) deals with the balance between work, childcare and eldercare.

CHAPTER 4

Organize Positively

"The key to change is not seeking to change other people. The key is seeking to create a relationship or community in which the other people can better flourish. This means increasing my commitment to the collective good."
—**Dr. Robert Quinn, University of Michigan**

No matter how much we increase our own positivity, it is difficult to succeed in an environment that does not support flourishing. This chapter explores the concept of positive organizing, a set of principles that serve to create a beneficial environment and a topic of conversation shared in a keynote by Dr. Robert Quinn at the Conference in 2012.

The work of Quinn and his colleagues—Dr. Kim Cameron, Dr. Jane Dutton and others—has led to a new business discipline called positive organizational scholarship, which was introduced in 2003. It is the study of practices that lead organizations to become positive places to work.[27]

This discipline draws on the fields of positive psychology, community psychology, positive organizational behavior and organizational development. It applies practices such as reflective action, appreciative inquiry, gratitude and mindfulness in the workplace. Positive organizing invites people to find their purpose, engages them in authentic conversation, empowers them to see possibility, focuses on the common good, and trusts the emergent process.[28]

Using the principles of positive organizing is an unconventional approach to leading, and is a path that many are afraid to even start. Yet, I am convinced that this is the only way (often combined with traditional forms of management, which Quinn calls "bilingual leadership") to see lasting change.

While organizational life that is stagnant or overwhelmingly busy can lead to downward cycles of depletion, as we discussed in Chapter One, Quinn explains how "positive organizing" can lead to a cycle of continual renewal, where employees are engaged and exceed expectations. I interviewed him about this concept and he told a compelling story of change that portrays each of the principles of positive organizing.

> We were approached by a large urban school district that was bankrupt and on their 4th Emergency Manager. The children were performing at 4% of State proficiency in some subjects. The problems and conditions were beyond imagination. It was a system where it would seem like the only solution would be to tear it down and start over again.
>
> They called Dr. Kim Cameron and me and said, "Can you help us?" We went and met with ninety of their principals. The new Emergency Manager gave a ten-minute talk that I thought was impressive, but there was almost no applause. People were totally uninvolved. Kim, my colleague, leaned over to me and said, "These people don't believe." And I said, "No kidding," because these people were making $10,000 less now than they were ten years ago. They felt like they'd been punished and burned.
>
> Kim got up and started presenting some of the concepts of positive organizing, and that's when the first miracle occurred. I noticed that they were leaning forward. Now, these are no-nonsense people. They know the difference between "noise" and something that matters, and they were paying attention. My antennae went up, and then

Kim asked a question. There were a few comments that brought tears to my eyes. The kind of tears I get when I have a spiritual experience. I could feel that these were people who felt abused by the system, but who got up every day anyway and went to work because they had a higher purpose. And that underneath all that pain was enormous authenticity. And I knew that those were the only two things we needed to succeed in a system where you would say there is no hope.

What Quinn was noticing was that two of the principles of positive organizing—creating a sense of purpose, and having authentic conversations—were possible with this group. The people were also starting to see that there was possibility of moving forward, through all the examples and the research that Dr. Cameron was presenting. Quinn then began to get the group involved in having a truly authentic conversation.

I got up and said, "I come here naked and I have no PowerPoint. I have no presentation prepared; I only have a set of questions to ask you." I asked them my questions, had them discuss them and then debriefed. There was a pretty impressive conversation that emerged, and it appeared to be a home run when one woman stood up and exclaimed, "I'm going to tell you like it is!" She was a principal and she started to speak of these extreme negative situations and people were yelling, "Go sister, go sister!" And she went on for a long time.

When she was done pouring out all this pain, I simply said "Why?" She said, "Why what?" And I said, "Why do you do it?"

She said, "That's what I signed up for." I said "No, that's not why you do it."

The room went dead quiet, ready to explode and it was a very dramatic moment. I just stood there and finally a man on the other side of the room said,

"It's the kids. You do it because of the kids."

And all the heads nodded. I said, "That's right, and that's why there is plenty of hope that can be engendered in this system; because every one of you are people of purpose. You feel abused, and have felt abused for ten years. You're doing things that are super-human, just getting to work in the morning, and the reason why you do it and you don't quit is because you care about the kids. Because of this there are things we can do here.

Engaging in this meaningful, authentic conversation helped them to remember their sense of purpose, and as the meeting went on they found a renewed sense of hope for the future. They began to focus again on the common good.

Later, the administrator that brought us in said, "That was so much better than I expected!" Now if you freeze that for a moment, that is a very important piece of input. The question we must ask is "what did he expect?"

What he expected is that we would get up and talk at them like everyone talks at each other, and for nothing to happen. Yet, something dramatic happened in that room. We were walking out and I ended up next to that same energized woman and she started in all over again—and then she stopped cold and she had an epiphany and she said, "That's it! Maybe in this huge transformation that requires a scapegoat, my role is to be a scapegoat. And you know what? I'm OK with that!" And her face changed, her body changed. She hugged me and she walked to her car.

A week later Quinn and Cameron met with the top people in the organization for two days and had similar conversations. From Dr. Quinn:

We opened up the extreme conversation where one of them said,

"I feel like I am married to an abusive husband, and my husband is the school district." All the hands in the room went up, and another woman said, "Yeah, me too." She said, "I know a lot of women in abusive marriages and there's a large subset of them that stay for the simple reason that if they stay, the kids get beaten less often," and she said, "that's why I stay at the school, because the kids suffer less than if I leave."

And another woman raised her hand and said, "And that raises a very significant question: can an organization full of abused people be a part of a transformation?" I listened to these questions until they were all out, and then I said, "Well, what are you going to do to answer these questions?"

They initially said, "We can't answer them."

I said, "Yes, you can, so let's talk about this." And eventually it turned into "why would we trust the Emergency Manager?" So we opened that question up and one of the women finally said, "because we have no choice. We can't afford to lose another generation of children. We have to trust him."

That was a pretty significant moment. The Emergency Manager stood up and said "What I've learned in the last two days is more powerful and meaningful and useful than anything I've learned in the past year, and what is clear to me is that I need to enlist the ninety of you as my transformation team. Every idea needs to be vetted through you, and you need to carry the ideas to the organization. I need you. How many of you would be willing to be on that team?"

This is a group of people who, two days before, were not impressed with this guy. Ninety hands went up.

In a relatively short period of time (two meetings) this group of people who had been suffering through dysfunction and lack of vision for years pulled together to create a new future. They had become re-engaged in their purpose, engaged in authentic conversations, empowered to see the possibilities, focused on the common good, and were trusting in the emergent process—all five of the principles of positive organizing.

> *That was nine months ago. There has been tremendous progress on one level, while there are still endless problems at another level. But the one thing they are trying to do in the face of those endless problems is to maintain a positive culture.*
>
> *The principal who poured out her story in our first meeting resolved to create a positive school, no matter what was going on. It's a very dramatic story. If an organization like that can make progress then any company can make progress. They began to trust in the emergent process and we moved together and co-created a new future. That's very different than having a technical solution to the problems.*

Positive organizing is now a well-studied, but not well-used, set of business principles. However, research keeps mounting to show how these principles can create environments where upward spirals allow continual renewal, which creates teams of people who exceed expectations. If your organization is one that is used to crisis management or conventional management practices, using the principles of positive organizing with your teams will require you to be positively deviant.

What practices can you implement that will be different from 'the way we've always done things' and lead to a better way to do business in the future?

In the process of breaking down the principles of positive organizing to better understand them, I asked Dr. Quinn for more background on each.

Finding Purpose

Quinn stresses the importance of allowing purpose to emerge as it did for the people in the school district. According to him, research shows that corporate purpose statements often do more harm than good because they are political exercises rather than words that people passionately believe in. This raises cynicism within the organization. He suggests these questions to determine if your purpose statement is real:

- For what would we sacrifice?
- If this is our purpose, then what things would we suffer inconvenience around because of it? (e.g. working night shifts)
- If this is our purpose, how will we relate to each other differently?
- Do the people immediately below me share this purpose?
- If they share this purpose, what sacrifices are they willing to make?

Continuing to ask these questions tests the authenticity of the purpose that is emerging. I asked him what methods he has found most useful to engage people in finding purpose:

The whole challenge from the very first moment is to maintain authenticity around the search for purpose, the statement of purpose, and then the process of communicating purpose. Using the questions [above] provides a constant testing of authenticity all the way through the process.

He stresses that purpose is not something that a senior person invents and announces, but rather something to discover.

It already exists, but no one can tell you what it is. You must go out and do the work that leads to the discovery of the process, and then establish relationships in which it is continually being discussed and tested, and that you're learning and they're learning in a co-creative process. This language is mysterious to the conventional managerial mind. What it suggests is that when we are creating together, we're learning together. We're equals. Meaning emerges in real time; purpose emerges in real time.

I found this "need to discover purpose" to be very true when leading the conference. We were into our 5th year before we solidified our mission and vision, and it wasn't until after our 10th year that our purpose statement emerged. It was a co-creative process in both cases.

In the beginning, I had a vision for a national conference and gathered together the right team who could put on an outstanding first few events. Over time however, it was important for the entire team to create our mission, vision and purpose for the future so that it became the mission of the group and we were all striving for the same vision.

The mission and vision were developed in our first off-site retreat, five years after starting the event. We began the retreat by watching Dewitt Jones' "Celebrate What's Right with the World" DVD.[29] This is an inspiring video that I use frequently with groups to shift them out of the conventional "problem-solving" mindset and into a "possibility" mindset.

We then discussed what we were doing right, what we were doing well, what we believed in, what we were all about, and what we aspired to be. We were using appreciative inquiry. We brainstormed, we had individual reflection time, and in the end we came up with a mission of *"creating extraordinary workplaces by developing extraordinary people,"* while our vision was *"to see workplace wellness become commonplace so that 'the extraordinary' becomes 'the expected.'"* These statements stood the test of time, staying in use for the remaining 12 years that we put on the conference.

A few years later, I felt we needed to define our purpose. We had new team members, and we needed to have this discussion again. The team was very passionate about what we were doing, and going through the exercise of developing a purpose statement helped to solidify the group even more.

I remember one discussion we had in my dining room during a retreat. We had flipchart papers all over the walls and we had a few statements that stood out. We were closing in on one, but I was feeling like we weren't there yet. Talking to no one in particular, I said, "That's just not quite it, because what we're really about is creating a better workplace." Our Marketing Director got excited and said, "That's it! That's our purpose! Creating a better workplace!"

It sounds so simple, and it really is, but it took time to emerge. This became the purpose of our organization going forward, eventually causing us to change the name of the conference from "The Health Work & Wellness™ Conference" to "The Better Workplace Conference."

Authentic Conversation

Engaging in authentic conversation is the second principle of positive organizing. In Quinn's process, he asks questions and tries to listen less to the content of what people are saying, and more to the passion with which they are saying it along with the non-verbal cues. As time goes on, he asks more penetrating questions to move the conversation toward a more authentic exchange "where people start to tell the truth, which doesn't normally occur."

I asked him if these were "transformational" questions. He responded:

> It can be any kind of question in that early stage. I remember talking to a woman in a company going through tremendous difficulty and just simply saying to her, "Can you tell me about the

pain you're feeling?" It went from a typical conversation to her bursting into tears and then on to express thoughts that had not been talked about. It can be any kind of question where you are picking up on the signals of what's really going on.

Quinn pointed out that this is not your conventional type of consulting. "Most people," he says, "try to create organizational change by engaging in traditional exchange-driven secular conversation, which often simply reinforces the problems."

Seeing the Possibilities

Several of the leaders I interviewed directed me to the research of Dr. Barbara Fredrickson, principal investigator of the Positive Emotions and Psychophysiology Laboratory at the University of North Carolina. Her career has been focused on studying how positive emotions lead to a greater sense of purpose, higher levels of psychological and social functioning, more engagement in work and transcendence from self-interest.

Dr. Fredrickson tells us that just as negative thinking narrows our views on possibilities, positivity broadens our minds to them.[30] In the school board example, it was an authentic conversation that helped people zero in on their purpose and opened possibility thinking.

As leaders, it is our job to help others see new realities. How can you encourage possibility thinking in your teams/organization? Practices that increase positive emotions are one way to open this line of thinking and unleash creativity and innovation.

One tool that Dr. Quinn uses to encourage possibility thinking is a tool he developed called the Positive Organization Generator (POG). This tool is explained in detail in his book, "The Positive Organization: Breaking Free From Conventional Cultures,

Constraints, and Beliefs," and a free version can be found online at a website called Lift Exchange®.[28,31]

The POG helps you to assess how positive your organization is and then provides a listing of 100 practices that are being used successfully in other organizations. The practices span all the principles of positive organizing. As I've stressed throughout this book, the key to successfully implementing practices that will make your organization flourish is not to try to simply replicate them, but to tailor and re-create the practices to fit your own unique culture and orientation.

In his week-long leadership retreats, Quinn asks participants what they are going to do differently because of the retreat, and he says "they get this terrified look in their eyes! I spend a lot of time working on that terrified look."

He explains that what is going on is that they have been introduced to these new positive practices that make sense. However, they may come from cultures that are macho, technical or political and they are trying to determine how to introduce positive practices without it being an embarrassment. Does this sound familiar? Quinn explains:

This fear of embarrassment is so powerful that it prevents change. It is very real. It's not just the people in the room; it's universal.

I began working on that. I run a contest, and every person in the room is asked to list the three most positive practices they can think of and then share the best one with their table. The table group picks the best one, and that person from each table gets to stand up and tell us what it is, while we have a panel of judges at the back doing Olympic voting from 1-10 on each, so someone wins. They have the best idea in the room and I give them a real prize for their work, and people have fun and they are enjoying these good ideas.

And then I say to them, in the next hour you must come up with three to five ideas that are better than the best idea that just won the prize. I give them the Positive Organization Generator and ask them to pick the ten ideas that are most interesting from the 100 ideas in the book. Then pick the three to five that are the most energizing, and re-invent them.

This is the key word: re-invent them to something that you believe will work for you. In fact, you believe it so strongly that no one could stop you from going back and trying. And the reason this is so important is because you must feel that way, so that when you go back and fail…as you will…you will have the resilience to keep going to learn how to implement that practice.

They go out of the room and they come back—and sure enough, they're just on fire when they come back because they have invented their own practices.

It is at this point that he says they are ready to go back to their workplace and do something that works. Without an exercise that makes them "own it, feel it, be passionate about it and be willing to fail in moving forward, learning how to do it, they would not be ready." This kind of exercise prepares people for change.

What can you do with your team or organization to help people see different possibilities, and be prepared to invent new practices that will work in your culture? How can you use the Positive Organization Generator to help you with this?

Focus on the Common Good

Focusing on the common good is about moving past our own self-interest and living by principle instead of following the status quo. To embrace the common good means to exercise moral power, the influence that comes when we make decisions based on principle rather than politics.[28] Many organizations have cultures of internal competition. People within the organization are competing for recognition and advancement, afraid to make mistakes that would cost them a promotion. There is enough research now to show that this kind of environment can hinder the creativity and innovation needed for breakthrough performance.

Exercising moral power and embracing the common good are positively deviant acts. They are the opposite of the conventional way of doing business that many of us were brought up in. Let's embrace them anyway.

When you act in positively deviant ways, and speak truth to power, the ripple effect causes others to think differently about their own choices. It creates "positive" peer pressure. Rising above self-interest and choosing to focus on the common good is called "pro-social motivation." The Oxford Handbook of Positive Organizational Scholarship says that "employees who are pro-socially motivated take initiative, persist in meaningful tasks, help others, enhance the well-being of others, strengthen cooperation and collaboration, are proactive and creative, perform better at work, are inspired, and have more energy."[32] What more could we ask for from employees?

Moving from a mindset of caring only about our own well-being to caring about the well-being of all is transformational leadership. This is essential for culture change.

The community I described in Chapter One that spontaneously developed through the first Conference, and then continued to grow through subsequent conferences, is an example of how a group came together and embraced the common good. This movement was not directed by any one person. It was a coming together of like-minded individuals who did not know each other prior to attending the first conference, but who quickly took ownership. They worked on committees, acted as ambassadors, joined us as on-the-ground volunteers who welcomed people, made connections for newcomers, ran fitness breaks, introduced speakers and played numerous roles to increase awareness and promote the concept of workplace health. I believe they were so engaged because they saw the need for workplace change, they believed in the vision and purpose of this movement and saw the possibilities that we could create. There were a great many people who stepped forward simply to work for the common good.

It was fascinating to watch as organizations who sponsored the conference did the same. There are many conferences that have only one sponsor from each industry because the others don't want to be involved in an event sponsored by their competitor. I often commented that many sponsors who competed "out there" came together "in here" to support the event. On certain years, we had every major insurance institution and every major employee assistance firm in Canada involved at the same time.

Internally, we also made decisions that were based on the common good versus individual gain. When the conference began, we chose to price it at approximately half of what a few similar events were charging, with the aim of making it as accessible to as many people and organizations as possible. Our *raison d'être* was to increase awareness about the benefits of workplace health and to create extraordinary organizations by developing the extraordinary people who were attracted to this event. As a result, our attendance numbers were higher than similar conferences.

With this focus on the common good, the Conference achieved its purpose of increasing awareness about organizational health. Along the way, it also created a well-connected community across the country and beyond. It stayed on the leading edge of workplace health research and practice, bringing together thought-leaders from around the world to share tools, strategies and practices.

If individuals and teams who have this orientation towards the common good perform better, are more creative and have more energy, it only makes sense to encourage this focus in our workplaces.

Trusting the Emergent Process

In our fast-paced, "I need results now" society, trusting that the results we want will emerge over time if we put the right practices in place is difficult. But, this is a necessary part of the process.

When we begin personal practices, such as asking transformational questions or examining our leadership hypocrisies, the results are not immediate. It is the same when embarking on positive organizational change and implementing team and/or organizational practices. As we practice and trust the emergent process, results develop on their own time and in different ways than we may have orchestrated. People tend to organize based on their knowledge and skills, and then work toward common goals in different ways than we may have imagined. Often the results will be even better than we expected.

As seen in the school board example, once the group felt they could trust the consultants, they were led to a place of re-connecting with their purpose, seeing the possibilities, and having a truly authentic conversation. They began to trust in the emergent process that would unfold, and that opened more conversation and more possibilities.

Dr. Quinn provided another example of how the emergent process worked with a different participant in his leadership course:

Recently we had a leader who went home, and based on that last exercise I do where they come up with their own practices, he decided to do nothing for three weeks when he got back. He spent the entire three weeks asking one question: "how can I take everything I learned in this course, and reduce it to one single act that would transform my organization?" That was incredibly impressive. It's a brilliant question. It's a question of commitment. And in fact, he spent three weeks doing this and he came up with his own answer.

He walked to the white board in his own office and wrote down "what result do you want to create?" Then when every direct report came in with a problem, he simply pointed at the white board. They thought he was crazy and they had difficulty making sense of it. But then something interesting started to happen—they started to walk in with their problems and their own answers, and once they answered he would talk with them and simply focus them back on their own answer. He said in a matter of three weeks he saw more change in his culture than he's ever seen. Now that is a brilliant story.

Higher performance is not just enhanced by a more positive work culture; it requires it. Now it is your turn. Based on these examples of positive organizing, and understanding the five principles, what practices can you develop or re-invent that will orient your team or organization in a positive direction? How can you use the POG to inspire you?

ACTIVITIES

Personal Practices:

1. Set a timer for five minutes and begin a focused writing exercise in your journal on this question: "One year from now, based on what I have read in this chapter, what positive characteristics would I like my team or organization to have?"

2. Take another five minutes to list the gaps between the future team or organization you desire to have and where you are now.

3. Based on what you have read in this chapter, what personal leadership practices can you adopt, customize and implement that will be different from "the way we've always done things" and lead to a better way to do business in the future?

Team Practice:

Consider the five principles outlined in this chapter: finding purpose, authentic conversation, seeing possibilities, focusing on the common good, and trusting the emergent process. Which area do you need to focus on first to shift your team in a more positive direction? Lead a discussion with your team about this.

For example, if finding purpose is your focus, lead a discussion with your team on your purpose using the following questions:

- For what would we sacrifice?
- If this is our purpose, then what things would we suffer inconvenience around because of it?
- If this is our purpose, how will we relate to each other differently?
- Do the people immediately below me share this purpose?
- If they share this purpose, what sacrifices are they willing to make?

Organizational Practice:

Fill in the following five quick assessments to get a rough idea of where your organization is, based on the five principles discussed in this chapter. These assessments are from "The Positive Organization"[28] and are used here with permission.

After you assess where your organization is on the five principles, either go to the POG in the appendices of "The Positive Organization" or go online to http://www.liftexchange.com/generator and review the 100 practices from positive organizations. Choose three practices that interest you based on where your organization or team needs to improve. Customize them to something that will work in your culture, or use them as inspiration to develop your own.

Add these to your through-line plan, implementing them when the time is right and course correcting as you go along. Be prepared for them to fail; learn from those failures and reinvent them until you find effective practices that will create positive change.

Quick Assessment on Purpose

On a scale of 1 to 10, assess which number most closely represents your opinion of where your organization is at in terms of finding purpose.

We work to make money	1 2 3 4 5 6 7 8 9 10	We work for a higher purpose
Our work lacks meaning	1 2 3 4 5 6 7 8 9 10	Our work has meaning
We lack a sense of shared purpose	1 2 3 4 5 6 7 8 9 10	We have a sense of shared purpose
We do what we are assigned to do	1 2 3 4 5 6 7 8 9 10	We do what we love to do
We do not get meaningful feedback	1 2 3 4 5 6 7 8 9 10	We get meaningful feedback

Quick Assessment on Authenticity

On a scale of 1 to 10, assess which number most closely represents your opinion of where your organization is at in terms of nurturing authentic conversations.

We only say what is politically correct	1 2 3 4 5 6 7 8 9 10	We say what we really feel
We do not treat each other with respect	1 2 3 4 5 6 7 8 9 10	We treat each other with respect
We avoid dealing with difficult issues	1 2 3 4 5 6 7 8 9 10	We constructively confront one another
We shoot down each other's ideas	1 2 3 4 5 6 7 8 9 10	We build off each other's ideas
We punish mistakes	1 2 3 4 5 6 7 8 9 10	We learn without blame

Quick Assessment on Possibility

On a scale of 1 to 10, assess which number most closely represents your opinion of where your organization is at in terms of seeing possibility.

We focus on constraints	1 2 3 4 5 6 7 8 9 10	We focus on possibilities
We are pessimistic	1 2 3 4 5 6 7 8 9 10	We are optimistic
We are reactive	1 2 3 4 5 6 7 8 9 10	We are proactive
We seek to solve problems	1 2 3 4 5 6 7 8 9 10	We seek to spread excellence
We are trapped in our own past	1 2 3 4 5 6 7 8 9 10	We are creating a new future

Quick Assessment on the Common Good

On a scale of 1 to 10, assess which number most closely represents your opinion of where your organization is at in terms of embracing the common good.

Leaders are pursuing their own self-interests	1 2 3 4 5 6 7 8 9 10	Leaders are pursuing the common good
We focus on our own personal needs	1 2 3 4 5 6 7 8 9 10	We focus on winning for the organization
We are operating in silos	1 2 3 4 5 6 7 8 9 10	We are all sacrificing for the shared vision
There is no desire to do a good job	1 2 3 4 5 6 7 8 9 10	The desire to do a good job is widespread
Negative peer pressure holds us back	1 2 3 4 5 6 7 8 9 10	Positive peer pressure moves us forward

Quick Assessment on Emergence

On a scale of 1 to 10, assess which number most closely represents your opinion of where your organization is at in terms of trusting the emergent process.

We are fearful of trying new things	1 2 3 4 5 6 7 8 9 10	We are empowered to try new things
We infect each other with cynicism	1 2 3 4 5 6 7 8 9 10	We infect each other with enthusiasm
Leadership is in one person	1 2 3 4 5 6 7 8 9 10	Leadership moves from person to person
We are micro-managed	1 2 3 4 5 6 7 8 9 10	We initiate without management direction
We fail to meet our own expectations	1 2 3 4 5 6 7 8 9 10	We exceed our own expectations

Featured Influencer: Dr. Robert Quinn

Robert E. Quinn

Robert E. Quinn is a professor emeritus at the University of Michigan's Ross School of Business. He is passionate about inspiring positive change and he continues to research, write, teach and consult.

He is one of the co-founders of the field of positive organizational scholarship and a co-founder of the Center for Positive Organizations. As an author, he has published 18 books. His best-selling volume, "Deep Change," is a tool for transformation. His book "The Best Teacher in You" won the Ben Franklin Award designating it the best book in education for 2015. The Harvard Business Review has selected his paper, "Moments of Greatness: Entering the Fundamental State of Leadership," as a classic and included it in their "10 Must Reads on Managing Yourself." He is currently working on a book tentatively titled, "You Cannot Create What You Cannot Imagine: Organizations and the Economics of Higher Purpose."

As a consultant, Quinn has 40 years of experience, and he is known for the competing values framework, a tool that is used by tens of thousands of managers. He is a fellow of the Academy of Management and the World Business Academy. He has received awards for both teaching and research. You can read more about Dr. Quinn on his website at www.bob-quinn.com and you can access his blog at thepositiveorganization.wordpress.com.

CHAPTER 5

Shift Yourself 1st

"A cynic, after all, is a passionate person who does not want to be disappointed again."
—**Rosamund Stone Zander and Benjamin Zander, The Art of Possibility**

Are you flourishing as a leader?

If I'm overextended and exhausted; if I'm late for every meeting because the one before it ran behind; if I'm sending emails through the weekend; whom am I serving? Who does it impact if, as a leader, I am not functioning at my best or embodying a healthy culture?

In the process of leading, we have a choice. We can have a culture that is busy and exhausting, or we can create a culture where continual renewal and resilience is possible. As Quinn explains in "The Deep Change Field Guide: A Personal Course to Discovering the Leader Within,"[33] it is impossible to expect organizational or team transformation unless you can change yourself.

> What change can you make personally to embody the culture that you want to see?

In this chapter, we explore evidence-based practices that help us maintain the energy, wellness and resilience to deal with the day-to-day and long-term challenges so we can succeed as leaders. We will also discover how to model and teach these habits in the workplace.

Finding your own way to flourish, and helping your team find theirs, is a great way to be positively deviant as a leader.

The downward cycle seen in many workplaces of being over-extended and exhausted results in decreased energy and increased negativity. As stress levels rise, creativity and innovation drop; as energy drops, we are more apt to misread communication from others and respond negatively.[33,34] Being in these cycles on a consistent basis can lead to burnout.

I received an email from a client once who was experiencing these symptoms. Mary said she was in a major burnout and had lost her ability to focus. She described the various big, exciting projects that were coming her way. She had been working very hard to create these and was passionate about them, but they had yet to launch and she was becoming financially strapped. She used phrases like, "I'm overwhelmed," "I can't sleep because of all of the thoughts that are running through my head," and "I feel like I'm not making a difference."

Although she used the words "major burnout," she was not recognizing her need to address it and instead was looking for technical solutions. Getting administrative help, prioritizing her tasks or delegating some of the work may have been helpful, but I was more concerned about her health as she was headed into a downward spiral. My first response to her is below.

Dear Mary,

I applaud you for reaching out with this. Hearing you say you are in major burnout leads me to urge you to STOP, step back and reflect. If you are truly burned out (exhaustion, cynicism, sleeplessness, feeling ineffective and unfocused), I hope you will slow down and address it so as not to experience a much longer burnout and recovery cycle.

I can speak about this personally since, like others in the helping professions, I have been through it. Not once—but twice. The first time, I took a bit of time off, recovered and then came back to work rested, wiser and much more mindful.

Twenty years later when it happened again, I denied it. I tried to push forward, thinking I would take the time later, once these projects were completed. I didn't want to admit I was there again, even though I was seeing all the signs. Once I knew, I didn't talk about it—even to those closest to me—and a year later I was still struggling. Had I taken the time when I first identified it, I am convinced I would have worked through it in a couple of months and been much further ahead.

You don't necessarily need to stop completely when you're slipping into burnout. But I suggest that you pick one project to focus on and put the others aside while you take the rest you need. Pick the one that brings you the most joy! I did this my first time around—I left the workplace behind, and just worked on one project.

Trust that these other projects will be waiting for you in a few weeks when a stronger version of you comes back; or, if they're not, others like them will be. Believe you will tackle them then, doing your best work versus doing the half-job that we do when we're burned out.

One of the books I've been reading is Brené Brown's "Rising Strong: The Reckoning. The Rumble. The Revolution."[35] What stood out to me the most from Brown's book was that "you can't skip the middle."

Burnout almost always starts with great excitement and opportunities such as you have in front of you (the beginning). The middle is where, as Dr.'s Maslach and Leiter point out, "energy turns to exhaustion, involvement turns to cynicism, and efficacy turns into ineffectiveness."[36] Projects pile up and we burnout. The end is when we come through it to a more sustainable place.

We tend to gloss over the middle piece, trying to get through it as fast as possible. But Brown says this is where we need to slow down, feel the discomfort, rumble with it, and acknowledge our feelings if we're going to learn from them. And then have those tough conversations with ourselves about how we really want our work life to feel.

As she says, "the middle is messy, but it's also where the magic happens."[35] My guess is that if you stop, pick one project and put the others aside while you rumble with what is happening, it will transform you and the work that you do into something even better. Brown says she's seen people go through this process in 20 minutes, and others take 20 years. If you don't want to be in the latter category... stop now.

When I went through my last run with burnout I made two lists. The first one was of things I would no longer do (like holding on to things past their usefulness). The second list was what I would continue or start doing (like practicing gratitude).

Mary, I know that what you were looking for was technical advice, but in my experience, we don't always ask for what we need most. I was reading a call for help of a different kind in what you had to say. I hope this is useful to you and that you put more than a Band-Aid on your burnout.

Sincerely,
Deborah Connors

Burnout

Maslach and Leiter called burnout a "barometer of a major social dysfunction in our workplace."[36] Dr. Leiter has spoken at the conference on a couple of occasions. His work with Dr. Maslach focuses on organizational behaviour and understanding burnout. They indicate that anger, cynicism and bitterness are the dominant emotions we see as symptoms.

What they described as a crisis two decades ago has become worse today, to the point where burnout is commonplace. In their book "Banishing Burnout: Six Strategies for Improving Your Relationship with Work," they call it the biggest occupational hazard of the twenty-first century.[37] Their research has uncovered many organizational practices that increase the likelihood of burnout, one of which is work overload. Couple this with lack of control, lack of reward, lack of community, lack of fairness or value conflicts, and the likelihood increases.

As leaders we can shift these practices, starting with our own behaviours. Rather than waiting until there are signs and symptoms of burnout to address, start creating a culture that rewards balance, fairness, and the values you espouse personally and organizationally.

Coming Back Strong from Burnout

Just as I experienced, the people who find themselves in burnout are often in denial about the symptoms. When we most need to be creative about the possibilities of how we can work differently, we become entrenched in our old ways of doing things and it can become a vicious cycle, as it was for Elizabeth in this next story.

She was in a situation where she was bullied; it was a unique situation because it was by someone reporting to her. Elizabeth describes this employee as being "toxic" to the system and very influential to others:

> *This story has changed my thinking and my approach as a leader. The situation led me into burnout, and as I came through it I became most interested in personal transformation.*
>
> *I have been in many leadership positions in my career and I know how to handle conflict, but all the things that I knew how to do weren't working in this situation. We had a very positive and healthy culture that turned negative through the actions and*

influence of one employee. It was like a toxic drop in the water that kept rippling and doing unbelievable damage.

As I look back on it now, I should have dealt directly and immediately with the root cause, but for many reasons I didn't. I have had to let people go before, and when I look back on those situations it was always the right thing to do. In this case though, there were many external pressures for our team to perform, and I was trying to help us succeed against all odds.

I thought I needed this person to continue because we were so understaffed, so I just figured I could make it work. There always seemed a justifiable reason to put off the difficult decision to let him go—I needed the work to get done, it was Christmas time and he had kids with medical problems, so I found a way to keep him on.

Most of us have probably been in these situations where we are understaffed and overcommitted. The situation escalated until other employees were quitting. Elizabeth explained how she didn't initially see how this was impacting her and the rest of the staff.

Had I let him go ten months prior, the situation would have been very different. It created the perfect storm. I didn't see that my stress level was rising to the point that I was also adding to the unhealthy culture. I was in survival mode and I thought I was managing my stress. Other people close to me could see it but I could not, and since I didn't deal with the source, it kept escalating.

Sometimes it takes getting to a place where you are completely dismantled to learn from it and rebuild from the ground up. I was wiped out. I had to let go of my job, I lost my confidence, I lost my energy, I started to drop into a depression—that sense of failure—and then I just had to recognize, "what was my role in it, and what would I do differently next time?"

I asked Elizabeth what she had learned through the process and what she is now doing differently. She talked about how she now owns her contribution to the issue and recognizes that she wasn't doing her staff any favours by keeping him on.

As a leader, you need to be critically aware of how your staff are affecting each other, but particularly how YOU are affecting people. Staff mimic and magnify the behaviour of their leader.

I would make the decision to let the person go faster. Often people enable a bad situation to continue thinking they are being empathetic. When you pass the point of empathy and you're enabling, you are affecting everyone in the organization. The most empathetic thing you can do for people sometimes is to let them go. When it's not a good fit, they suffer too. As a leader, you must make these decisions. We have lots of reasons why we don't do it—but it is our job.

I've also learned to recognize sooner when I've reached a place where I need to ask for help, or when I need to step aside. I see trouble coming much faster, which allows me to do the right thing sooner.

I now recognize sooner when to stop persisting and start quitting. It is critical to put your own oxygen mask on first. I am now more aware of my own motivations and triggers, and notice when symptoms arise.

You must be people-focused, versus solely focused on organizational goals. In the organization I am in now, I invest as much time in the people as I do into organizational outcomes. They want to contribute and do the work for you—but it starts with the leader."

Elizabeth went on to tell me how she brought what she learned from this situation to her next organization and how she developed a great team culture there. Her learnings are simple reminders for each of us as we support ourselves and others through similar situations:

- Own your contribution to the situation.
- Recognize when you need to ask for help.
- Let people go when it is not a good fit for the culture. Do this sooner.
- Put on your own oxygen mask first.
- Recognize when you are moving from empathy to enabling.
- Know when to quit.
- Focus on the people as well as the organizational goals.

Whether you've experienced burnout or you're coming back from some other setback, working through it requires stopping, reflecting and asking some transformational questions. What can I let go of? What brings me joy? What practices help clear and calm my mind? How can I best work through "the middle" and come out a better version of me?

These questions invite curiosity. Brown calls curiosity a "deviant" act because it changes our brain chemistry. When we feel the discomfort, and ask these tough questions about how things need to change, we can choose to end our stories differently.

Your Resilience Wardrobe

What can we take from our own experiences of slipping into burnout and from these shared stories? How do we create well-being and resilience personally and create wellness-focused cultures where we can one day banish burnout?

Rosamund Zander was a keynote speaker for the 2006 conference. I remember her sharing a saying from her father-in-law, which was "there is no such thing as bad weather, just inappropriate clothing!"

Building personal resilience is like having the appropriate clothing for any kind of weather—the storms, the conflicts, and the downward spirals that can sometimes occur in work situations. As leaders, we can think of practices as being the appropriate clothing, and a transformational leadership skill is knowing to use them on ourselves first (like putting on your oxygen mask first) when things get rocky.

What is in your resilience wardrobe? What can you pull out when needed to protect you from going on that downward spiral toward exhaustion and burnout as you walk through the storms?

Here are a few suggested leadership practices that can personally help maintain energy levels, and can also be used with teams or promoted organizationally:

1. Develop resilient cycles
2. Know what to let go of, continue and start
3. Break for energy
4. Be email intelligent
5. Disconnect
6. Develop better sleep habits

This next section describes what these leadership practices are and shares stories of how to integrate them into your own leadership style.

Develop Resilient Cycles

A funny thing happened when I was completing this book. I was behind schedule and found myself working into my summer vacation with houseguests and family commitments. Rather than putting it aside until a later date, I fell into my typical pattern of trying to meet the deadlines by writing late at night while on vacation.

So once my family had all gone to bed at 10:00 or 11:00 at night, I would get out my writing and sit down for two to three hours to work. I work well at night, and this pattern is OK in the short term, but as it carried on for weeks I started to look exhausted, feel sleep-deprived and become very ineffective. My own agenda was creating a "crisis" for my team, who were pushing me to meet the timelines so that they could succeed in helping me achieve this agenda! Can you see the vicious cycle here?

I looked in the mirror one morning and said, "Whoa!" Considering what I was writing about made it even more ironic; I needed to follow my own advice and say, "Let's stop, step back and have some breathing room." The book has been better for the extra time.

We all get caught in vicious cycles. In a class I took with author Patti Digh, she suggested creating our own cycles of resilience, which she calls virtuous circles.[38] This is a great exercise to examine the places you get stuck in vicious downward cycles and to visualize new, more resilient cycles.

During the course, I found myself sketching out one of my own vicious cycles in relation to my health and work style, shown in Diagram 4. When things in our lives are relatively calm, it is easy to maintain healthy work habits. It's when a crisis hits that we can find ourselves falling into bad habits, that lead to more bad habits, which can become a vicious cycle.

In my example, my old habit when the going got tough was to work harder, not smarter. This leads to being exhausted and overwhelmed, which can lead to not getting enough rest, eating poorly and practicing other bad habits, which make me feel worse.

The resilient cycle I sketched out to counteract this now causes me to stop myself when I start falling into these habits, and to consciously practice healthy habits that make me more effective in a lesser amount of time.

DIAGRAM #4 Vicious and Resilient Cycles

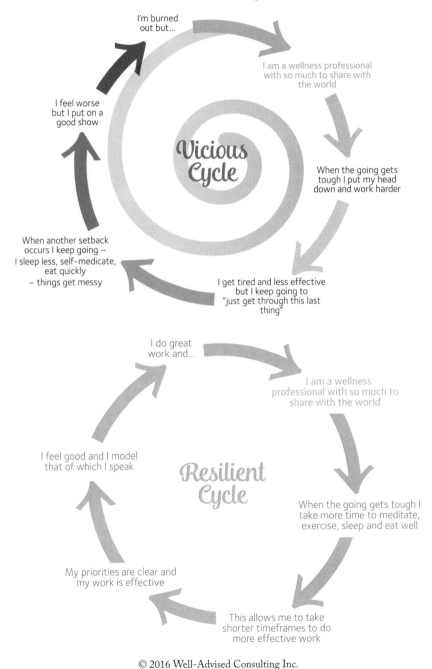

© 2016 Well-Advised Consulting Inc.

What are your vicious cycles? In what ways do you participate in cycles that make you more ineffective as a leader or negatively impact your health? In the activities at the end of this chapter there is an opportunity to draw your own vicious and resilient cycles.

Let Go, Continue and Start

During my recovery from burnout, I made a list of all the things I didn't want to do any longer. These were unsustainable patterns that led to exhaustion and unhappiness, and are barriers to flourishing. A few of the patterns on that list are:
1. Holding on to things past their usefulness.
2. Living by other people's agendas.
3. Letting other people's crises become my own.
4. Saying yes when I needed to say no.
5. Taking on a victim role.
6. Getting stuck.

Viewing this list, I see a pattern of giving up control and energy to others. Just creating a list like this will help you reflect on the aspects of your life that take you down into burnout.

I made another list of patterns that help me to flourish; ones that I focus on regularly. As the saying goes: "Focus on the part of your garden you want to grow the strongest!" This is a much more inspiring list. It makes me happy just to look at it. On this list are habits like:
1. Creating the time and space for my priorities.
2. Meditating daily.
3. Moving my body and building flexibility, cardiovascular health and strength.
4. Saying yes to being on time.
5. Practicing gratitude.
6. Reframing life's challenges.

7. Enjoying time with family and friends.

What is on your list of habits to stop or let go of? What about the ones that you will continue, or even start? How do you stay on track with these plans and not fall back into old patterns?

In the activities at the end of this chapter there is an opportunity for you to make your own lists to help you flourish. Having those lists is an important step in catching yourself when you start going into one of your old vicious cycles.

Break for Energy

It happened again. I was working hard on a project and thought I didn't have time to stop. "I'll just push through and get it done," I said, even though I knew better. (You saw my cycle above—this is my pattern!) Never mind all the research that says more hours doesn't equate to more productivity. I am aware of the studies that show how frequent breaks sustain your energy throughout the day, and I know first-hand how disconnecting and clearing my mind at just the right time can lead to brilliant breakthroughs. But instead of applying this knowledge, I put my head down and kept working, getting those emails out and doing my writing.

A glance at my schedule reminded me of an upcoming lunch hour Zumba class. At the last minute I made a break for it, running out the door, jumping in my car, heading for the gym and rushing into the packed room of women dancing to Latin beats. What a release is was to dance off that morning buildup of stress! I let the music and the sweat take over. An hour later I was back at my desk better than ever, head clearer, ideas rampant; I was reminded once again of how important it is to take that break.

The trend we're experiencing in North America where people work 10–12 hour days and take few breaks is not working well. Not only are we underutilizing people (exhausted people don't perform as well) and seeing an increase in burnout, but study after study show that this way of working does not help productivity.

We had a speaker from The Energy Project at the Conference in 2005 who told us that many of our beliefs about performance are incorrect. The Energy Project, started by CEO Tony Schwartz, reports that people who take frequent breaks have more focus and higher self-reported health and wellness.[39] Working too much without renewal also drains the cognitive resources we need to control our behaviours, desires and emotions.[40]

The Draughiem Group conducted research to show that our energy is affected more by the breaks we take within a work day than by the length of the day itself.[41] By studying different work patterns, they found that those who took short breaks regularly were more productive overall. The ideal ratio was found to be 52 minutes of focused work followed by a 17-minute break, which apparently follows the ebbs and flows in our brain energy; it allows us to work when our brain is most productive, and rest when it is least productive. The break allows our brains to refresh and be ready for another 52-minute focused session. People who take these breaks spend less time looking at distractions such as email or Facebook; studies also show that taking time to refresh allows us to be more productive in the long run versus having our energy diminish mid-afternoon.

Schwartz reminds us that energy is a renewable resource and that there are ways to use it more efficiently. He and other experts recommend shortening our focused work time and including more frequent breaks. In the work phase, just focus on work (which is easier to do when the timeframe is shorter). In the rest phase, do things that truly allow you to rest and renew.

Travis Bradbury—an Emotional Intelligence Expert, author and contributor to Forbes Business Magazine—suggests that since we are used to planning hourly, that we should continue to plan our workdays in one-hour chunks. This strategy keeps with the 52-minute focused time, which is then followed by eight minutes of rest.[42]

Although I know of no studies that have tested this method, I've tried it and I agree that it works well. I set a timer for 52 minutes and focus entirely on a project (staying off email and social media), and then when the timer goes I try to take an eight-minute break. Although it is tempting to keep going if you are really immersed, being respectful of the break (to walk, talk to someone or read) helped people in the Draughiem Group study to be more productive in their next work-session. Going online or texting was self-defeating as it did not provide the brain the same rest. I schedule in my time for email as a limited part of my focused work time.

What are your work and rest patterns? What can you do differently to conserve your energy?

Email intelligence

Xerox Canada was one of the front-runners in addressing the extra workload that email was creating for their employees. Back when we were just beginning to tackle this notion, Sacha Fraser from Xerox came to speak at the Conference in 2007 on their "Take Back the Hour" program. What they had realized was that people were spending an extra hour at work each day just responding to emails. They were one of the first organizations to develop individual, departmental and organizational guidelines for email use to curb that extra time.

For most, this problem continues to worsen. I read recently in Arianna Huffington's book, "Thrive," that people with smart phones check them, on average, every 6.5 minutes. This adds up to 150 times per day![43]

Aside from the extra time that email takes, it also has other negative effects. A 2014 UBC Study by Dunn & Kushlev reports that checking emails frequently causes more stress, among other issues, releasing more cortisol into our systems which then interferes with memory and lowers immunity.[44]

In my interview with Dr. Linda Duxbury, whose research has focused on work-life balance, she gave some recommendations about the email issue:

We need to have discussions. When phones first came out, people would listen on party lines because that was entertaining, and we had to come up with etiquette and rules around what was appropriate phone use.

We have not done that with email. One of the things I strongly believe is that we need to establish a set of protocols that govern email use. You shouldn't feel that if you're not on email 24/7 your career will suffer.

Every organization needs to do this individually.

President of Inside Health and Business Consulting Mary-Lou MacDonald also stressed the importance of leading by example with this issue during our interview:

I do not look at or respond to work emails on the weekend. I will only check if there is a rare exception that requires me to. As a leader, if I were to respond it would establish expectations and patterns.

Some research suggests that in addition to evening limits for email, you should also limit yourself throughout the day to only checking email at three specified times. After that surge of cortisol caused by checking your email, a relaxation response is activated in between. As a result, longer periods between checking email allow for less cortisol and more relaxation.

I have found that checking email just three times per day is useful when I'm in the office. I try to use the hours of 9:00 AM, 12:00

and 3:00 PM to do this, spending only ten minutes each time to respond. Anything that requires a longer response is worked into my schedule for later.

Christina Cavanagh, author of "Managing Your Email: Thinking Outside the Inbox,"[45] keynoted at the Conference in 2007, which had a theme of "Conquering the Chaos." After listening to her, our Conference Team implemented some of her suggestions on how to more effectively use our email. We developed guidelines on who to copy and not copy. We also adopted the idea of using EOM (short for End of Message) at the end of a subject line if that line was the entire message, indicating that the reader did not need to open the email. We started thinking and acting much more carefully with our email use.

What conscious decision can you make today to be email intelligent? How can you develop shared guidelines within your workplace to reduce email stress?

Disconnect

As I suggested to Mary, sometimes we just need to stop, reflect and then act. As a society, we are more geared toward action than reflection. A continual state of "busyness" doesn't allow for renewal and focused decisions.

Vacations or longer periods of disconnection are as important as those small, daily breaks. When there was no email, smartphones or WiFi connections in hotels, people used to take real vacations. I was one of those people! I'd go for two to three weeks somewhere with no phone or email. Nowadays this disconnection is out of the ordinary.

I completely disconnected on a recent three-week vacation to Greece. As my mother and I were hiking up the steps to see the Acropolis, we were taking pictures and considering that this place was the birthplace of democracy. Suddenly, I noticed there was a man behind me checking his emails on his phone! He was talking to his friend about his work that he'd carried with him to this spectacular spot. His friend said, "I can't believe you're checking your emails," to which the man replied, "I have to. Otherwise I'll come home to 4000 of them!"

I was sad that he was missing the moment, but I also recognized his thought process. A decision to disconnect on vacation may take a lot of planning to reduce the overwhelm of sifting through thousands of emails on your return. However, there are strategies you can use to help you disconnect while you are away. One strategy used by Duxbury is her bounce-back message that shares her return date and asks people to email her again after that time if it's important, deleting the incoming message.

I used this strategy on my vacation. The world didn't end. A two-to-three week get-away, completely disconnected from work, does wonders for becoming refreshed, reducing stress, increasing energy and gaining perspective. We simply must stop occasionally, slow down, work less, breathe more, step away and reflect. Then we can come out the other side rested and with more attention, creativity, proactivity and possibility!

Another approach is to start with small changes as you plan how you will disconnect or take a vacation. Ron Friedman, an award-winning psychologist and author, suggests making some minor adjustments to behaviour, such as leaving your phone in another room when you get home from work.[46] Instead of trying to change everything at once, find one small change you can implement right away and build on that. For example, before my vacation I started leaving my phone at home on purpose when I would go out somewhere, just to get used to being without it!

When I asked Mary-Lou MacDonald what practices she uses for disconnecting, she talked about activities that require mind-body connection.

In the work I'm in, I'm in my head a lot. Disconnecting, through practices that use the body-mind connection (like pilates or running), allows me to drop back into my body and get grounded. It requires me to be focused on the appropriate movement or on my breath. It links body-mind and gets me out of my head. It's the physical and mental connection removed from work.

I get the same sense of disconnecting that Mary-Lou is talking about when I'm skiing on the mountain. Each turn requires such focus and mindfulness that I can't be thinking about work. I'm right there, in the moment, focused on my next move and completely disconnected from work. A day on the mountain feels like a complete vacation to me.

What can you do on a daily and weekly basis to disconnect from work for periods of time? How can you plan your next vacation to be a complete and refreshing disconnect from work?

Develop Better Sleep Habits

The extra time we spend at work, as well as being connected to work, must come from somewhere. The Division of Sleep Medicine at Harvard Medical School[47] says that most people are making up this time by sleeping less. We treat sleep as a luxury instead of as a necessity, and they warn that as a society most of us do not get enough.

Research is showing that in the short term, getting an insufficient amount of sleep affects judgment, mood, learning and information retention, as well as increasing the risk of accidents. In the long term, it increases our risks of several chronic diseases including diabetes, obesity and cardiovascular disease. Sleep deprivation has been shown to have been a significant factor in oil spills, nuclear disasters and medical errors. It reduces our ability to focus and to access higher-level cognitive functions such as reasoning.

The Division of Sleep Medicine cites a 2004 study led by Dr. Charles Czeisler, which shows that medical errors could be reduced by as much as 36% by reducing the maximum shift for a doctor on call to 16 hours (versus 24-36 hours in some places) and by setting a maximum of 80 hours per work week for medical staff.

Mary-Lou MacDonald talked about sleep habits and what she does personally to stay on top of her game:

I have found that to perform at work, sleep hygiene is essential. If you think about the example of an Olympic athlete, they don't show up at the Olympics without preparation. Creating and supporting a healthy workplace is also a 24-hour job. To reach my potential, what I do at home counts before I even head to work.

Sometimes people think they can squeak by without paying attention to this, but I witness people dragging themselves around and being cranky because they're tired. They think they're entitled to be this way, but I believe it is disrespectful to those around you. As a leader, it is your responsibility to set an example for your staff. It's so important to be positive and turn every situation around the best you can.

The more sleep I get before midnight the better I feel the next day, so I try to head to bed around 9:00 with the intention of being asleep by 10:00. I use the time in between for my "wind-down" routine, which includes a combination of reading, journals, prayer or whatever is quiet and comforting for me. I have eliminated TV from the bedroom and I pay way more attention to my diet, alcohol and caffeine intake.

I have recently added earplugs and an eye mask to my wardrobe! Although admittedly not very attractive, they have exponentially increased my sleep quality and quantity, especially when I am in hotels. Having suffered serious bouts of insomnia in the past, I now have the utmost respect for my sleep and make it a priority. When

I feel rested, I have the capacity to handle anything that comes my way the next day and make the best of it.

You can fill yourself with so much noise that you don't have a sense anymore of what is real or what is imagined. I took some time recently to really get quiet and listen to my response to everything. It is a 24/7 analysis of life and what helps me bring my best self to everything I'm doing, and I find I am constantly trimming my sails.

Are you getting enough sleep? What step can you take today to improve your sleep habits?

Promoting a More Resilient Culture at Work

Creating a culture of continual renewal is not the norm in our society. It is a positively deviant choice that starts with self-transformation. If you want to have high productivity and creativity at work, it is the only choice. Without renewal, we increase the risk of finding ourselves in vicious downward spirals and even experiencing burnout.

The leadership practices we've just discussed—developing resilient cycles, letting go of that which no longer serves us, breaking for energy, finding ways to be email intelligent, disconnecting from work and developing better sleep habits—can transform us and our workplaces to be more resilient. Finding ways to recognize and reward balance, fairness and community within our organizations will also increase the likelihood of resilience and decrease the likelihood of burnout at work.

Try the practices below to start building a culture of personal, team and organizational renewal.

ACTIVITIES

Personal Practices:

1. When the going gets tough, are there unhealthy patterns that you fall into? In what ways do you become more ineffective, and does that lead to even more ineffectiveness? What are the vicious cycles you fall into? Use the cycle below to add your own words.

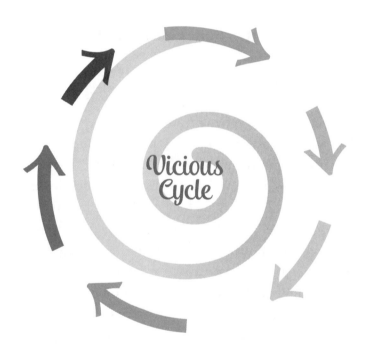

Now, try turning your vicious cycle around by drawing a resilient cycle for yourself. What healthy work practices can you focus on or develop to create a more effective cycle for yourself?

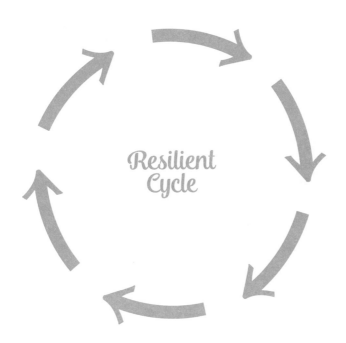

2. Based on your own habits and the practices discussed in this chapter, make a list of at least five things you will stop doing (or let go of), continue doing (build on) and start doing to create continual renewal for yourself.

STOP/LET GO   CONTINUE/BUILD ON   START

_____   _____   _____

_____   _____   _____

_____   _____   _____

3. What are your next three turns to create continual renewal, both personally and for your team/organization? Where do these fit in your through-line (i.e. This week, this month or in your someday plans)?

Team Practice:

Discuss with your team how you can be more email intelligent. What guidelines can you set up to reduce time on email? Discuss as a group how you take breaks, and how breaking for energy may help your team become more effective. Develop a set of practices to follow.

Organizational Practice:

Consider the following questions. Spend some time reflecting on them and make some notes in your journal.

- What are the values in your workplace? Do they need to be revisited?
- How do you reward people for living these values?
- If there is a mismatch between what your organization rewards and what the values are, what question do you need to ask and to whom to get that conversation started?

Featured Influencer: Mary-Lou MacDonald

Mary-Lou MacDonald

Mary-Lou started her career as a wellness specialist for elite athletes and coaches, and has been a visionary thinker and national authority in the field of workplace wellness for over 25 years. As an educator, practitioner, researcher, consultant, coach and speaker, she helps leaders create healthy cultures at work that translate into total well-being and high performance for themselves, their teams and their business.

As President of Inside Health and Business Consulting with a focus on organization health planning, she works with clients to implement strategies and build programs that support and maximize employee well-being, psychological safety, engagement and productivity. She speaks regularly and with compassion and vision about workplace mental health and the new National Standard for Psychological Health and Safety in the Workplace.

Mary-Lou most recently served as the Director of Workplace Health, Wellness and Safety Research at the Conference Board of Canada where she established the first ever benchmarking report on organizational health in Canada. She was the founding CEO of the Nova Scotia Health and Community Services Safety Association and served as Executive Director Atlantic, for Excellence Canada.

Mary-Lou has contributed many articles to scientific and other publications, including the Chronicle Herald, Journal of Applied

Physiology, Canadian HR Reporter, Healthcare Papers and Qmentum Quarterly.

You can find her at www.maryloumacdonald.com.

CHAPTER 6

Ignite Positivity

"No matter how good you are at negativity, you're also capable of positivity."
—**Dr. Barbara Fredrickson**

When you walk into an organization that has a positive culture, you can feel it immediately. A couple of decades ago I was volunteering as a Lead Assessor with the National Quality Institute (now Excellence Canada) to assess organizations who had applied to win the "Canada's Healthy Workplace Award." I remember walking into a big office tower of one of the companies vying for the award and immediately feeling like this was a great place to be. People were smiling and laughing. The energy was palpable. It seemed to be flourishing, and any questions we asked randomly to various employees were met with enthusiasm. What we learned through the assessment was that people did succeed in this environment, and it ended up being one of the organizations that won an award that year.

How do we invite flourishing into our workplaces, and why is this necessary? Dr. Michael West gives us two great reasons why striving to create this kind of organization makes good business sense. For one, he says, it is so much easier to manage an organization that is flourishing. Secondly, they perform better. He has conducted research on team and organizational innovation, much of which has been done with the UK National Health Service. They have shown overwhelming evidence that **the more positive the culture in the organization, the better it will perform**.

Understanding Positivity

Dr. Barbara Fredrickson has published many scholarly papers and books on positivity, including "Positivity: Top-Notch Research Reveals the Upward Spiral That Will Change Your Life" which provides numerous practices that increase positive emotions.[48] There is a body of research from Fredrickson and others that support the simple concept that as we increase positive emotions in our lives, we build personal resources in all the dimensions of optimum wellness—mental, physical, psychological, emotional and social. These resources include improved sleep, improved relationships with others, increased mindfulness and even reduced symptoms of illness.

A meta-analysis of 300 studies of positivity that followed 275,000 people showed that positivity both produces and reflects success in life.[49] As positive emotion increases it both broadens and builds, meaning we see more possibilities and one practice builds on another. We become more creative, resilient, engaged, optimistic and healthy, and we gain a sense of purpose. Evidence shows that positivity releases oxytocin and progesterone in the brain, which broadens perspective over time and improves our awareness, temporarily allowing us to take in more information about what is going on around us. It increases the amount of dopamine and opioids released into our system and reduces blood pressure.

All of this research helps explain the upward spirals presented by Fredrickson, which help us function at a high level and exceed expectations.

Is this not what we want in our workplaces?

Diagram 5 shows the upward spirals that are created as we participate in practices that increase positive emotions. It also shows the downward spirals that negative practices and emotions can bring on.

DIAGRAM #5 Individual Impact of Positive Workplace Practices

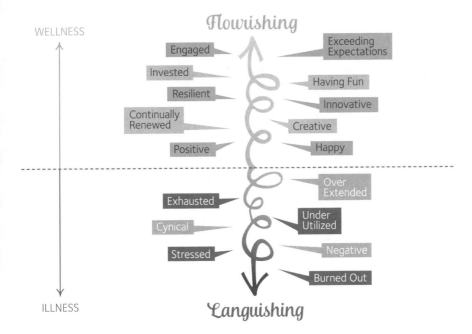

Downward Spirals

Downward spirals begin to occur when negative emotions, such as fear, narrow our view. In survival situations, this "fight or flight" response is helpful. For example, if your house is burning down, you want to narrow your options and get out. You don't want to sit and reflect on all the possibilities available to you in this situation.

This narrowing effect was important for survival for our ancestors—they only had one choice to make when being attacked by a large animal: do I fight or flee? Unfortunately, research shows that the same narrowing of available options occurs when we experience negative emotions that are not life-threatening. If we're in a stress-based or fear-based culture, our instinct is to fall back on that fight or flight mentality, which reduces creativity and productivity. If this type of culture is maintained, it leads us to languishing. This is the opposite of what individuals, teams and organizations need to succeed.

Downward spirals can be brought on by the way organizations operate and by the cultures that develop within them, and we can also go into negative spirals through our own thinking. I once met a very talented artist who had been painting all his life, but who was just now going into this profession full time and beginning to get showings in galleries. His work was stunning.

However, in one conversation he shared with me that some mornings he would get up and talk himself completely out of getting to work. The voices in his head would tell him he was no good, that he was wasting his time and ask him questions like "who do you think you are, trying to be an artist?" This would pull him into a downward spiral that sometimes prevented him from even getting into his studio that day.

Looking at the incredible talent in front of me, I couldn't believe that he could doubt himself. But then I recognized that line of conversation as one that I had participated in as well, and realized that we all do this at times. Sometimes when a negative incident happens, it sets us off and we invest in all the bad things that can happen in life. We start to get fearful and then one thought leads to the next, pulling us down.

Quinn and Cameron show that in organizational cultures where stress, anxiety, fear, sustained over-work and exhaustion are high, downward spirals lead to low productivity, less creativity, lower engagement and slow death in the organization.[50,51] The missing link could be to increase positive emotions in a workplace, which have a significant impact on outcomes. Old management styles do not take emotion into account, but as Quinn notes in his June 1, 2016 blog:

The fact is that emotions are real. Feelings of sadness, fear, anger, irritation, scorn, contempt, embarrassment, guilt, and shame determine behavior. They create the culture in which everyone must live and work, and less than optimal performance is associated with such emotions [52]

He says that good leaders understand this, and they work to implement practices that impact emotions in a positive way for themselves, their teams and their organizations. As positive emotions like appreciation, trust, compassion, confidence and hope start to surface, research shows that performance also improves.

The Negativity Bias

We've all been there. The day starts out fine, a few positive things happen, and then bang! There's this one phone call or interaction with someone and it sends us down a spiral, ruining the rest of the day.

Why is this? Dr. Barbara Fredrickson explains that we all have a negativity bias. Even though we have more positive experiences and thoughts than negative ones, the negative ones have more impact. Our brains tend to focus more on the negative than the positive, again apparently due to our evolution where a negative emotion was helpful in setting off the fight or flight response for survival. So, bad thoughts and emotions tend to trump good ones. And it is for that reason that working to increase the ratio of positive to negative emotions is the key to increasing our overall positivity, and to reaping the benefits that come with it.

How to Increase Positive Emotions and Create Upward Spirals

You will have also experienced times when you've felt on top of the world. Something good happened and you have positive emotions around it, so you get energized and create more positive emotions, which then makes you become more creative and the cycle continues going upward. As mentioned earlier, Fredrickson says this cycle increases our awareness and allows us to see more possibilities.

Increasing positivity is not about thinking positive; instead, it's about some very specific evidence-based practices that can be developed to increase positive emotions. A strong body of research shows that aiming for a minimum positivity ratio of 3:1, meaning that we have at least three positive thoughts or feelings for every negative one, which increases our likelihood of flourishing. Those individuals and teams with higher positivity ratios tend to flourish, and those with lower ratios tend to languish.[53,54]

Quinn uses the positivity ratio concept in a week-long course for executives he and Cameron teach, which draws on a wide body of evidence from positive psychology and positive organizational scholarship. From Dr. Quinn:

> *The positivity ratio is one of many concepts that we bring to executives. They are very cynical in the first two hours, and then they "get it" and they just soak it up.*
>
> *There is so much work that has implications for culture change and increased performance. In the course, Kim Cameron shares study after study about how positivity ratios work. The executives object. Then he shares more studies. Eventually they realize that these notions are not arbitrary. They're well documented principles.*
>
> *Then I usually start talking about organizational problems they normally never would talk about. We hold those up against these positive studies and the lights start to go on. What we do is what transformational leaders do—we're holding their hand and supporting them, while on the other hand we're holding a carrot way above their heads and constantly challenging them. So, it's challenge and support—which creates the context wherein they can begin to change. It's not challenge. It's not support. It's challenge AND support. It's task and person. It's integration."*

Whether or not we know the precise tipping point for people, we know that at a certain point of negativity we get pulled into a downward spiral. When you start to feel this tug, there are practices that will help you course-correct or, better yet, prevent the downward spiral altogether.

You can find practices in Diagram 6 which help increase positive emotions, including mindfulness, gratitude, reframing, and meditation. This next section describes these specific leadership practices and how to integrate them into your own leadership style.

DIAGRAM #6 **Workplace Practices That Promote Flourishing**

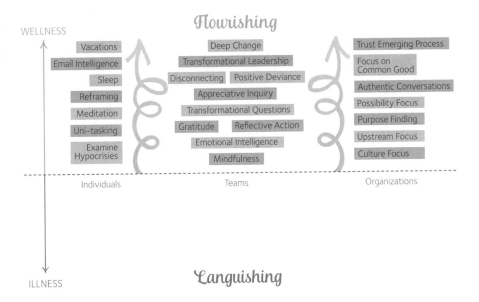

Mindfulness

I was writing this chapter while out on the wild West coast of Vancouver Island in Ucluelet. Here, when the sun shines it is the most beautiful place on earth; when it rains, it rains sideways. My only responsibility in exchange for staying in this peaceful and quiet house was to walk my brother and sister-in-law's dog Charlie while they were away.

One night it rained so hard that Charlie wouldn't even step outside the next morning, but I remembered that this was the day I had to put the garbage out. So, I pulled on my rubber boots and my brother's big Gortex hooded jacket, and out went the garbage. Charlie, realizing that the rain had lightened, was now looking eager to go. I grabbed a travel mug of coffee and off I went down the trail after her.

Mindfulness was on my mind, and I decided to make this my mindfulness walk. I have a friend who walks this way for an hour every morning along the ocean. It is his meditation, and he says it completely transforms his day. My previous walks by the ocean on this trip had been with another friend and her dog, so they were full of conversation. On my only other solitary morning walk here I was continually thinking I'd meet a bear (never mind that it was January and they were probably all hibernating) or that I'd get lost on the trail. Now I had realized this dog was a local, and I just needed to let her lead. So, that's what I did. I asked, "Which way, Charlie?" And I followed, and noticed.

The rain had stopped but the waves were bigger than ever, crashing into the rocks. The rain forest I walked through was full of every bright shade of green you can imagine. My mind would start wandering off, as they do, and I would pull it back to the present and be mindful of every step, every sight, every smell and every sound. I heard the call of a bird I'd never heard before and glanced up to see him. I saw an enormous eagle circling above—the reason for his cry. It was a magnificent, mindful walk, different than any other I had taken here during the week. And my day was much more positive and productive because of it.

As I begrudgingly pulled on my jacket and boots that morning to head out in the rain, little did I know how attentive this walk would be and how beneficial it would be to my day. I'm so grateful to Charlie that I didn't miss it.

What is Mindfulness?

How many things are you doing right now? Are you mindfully reading this chapter, or are you having lunch while you read? Are you thinking about tomorrow's deadline and checking emails and texts as they come in? Mindfulness is a simple process of tuning into what is around us and being aware of how we are responding to it, and it's a place we spend far too little time. This is unfortunate because we then miss out on the abundance of benefits that it can have on our health, positivity, work performance, and engagement in life, as well as on the cultures within which we work.

Barbara Frederickson and numerous other researchers recommend developing a mindfulness practice as a way of increasing the positive emotions in your life and curbing the downward momentum that comes with negative ones.

Dr. Jon Kabat-Zinn and Dr. Ellen Langer were two of the first researchers to study the psychology of mindfulness in North America.[55,56,57] In the early eighties, Kabat-Zinn developed a practice called Mindfulness-Based Stress Reduction that helps people to increase immune function and manage chronic pain, stress and anxiety. His study of over 4,000 people who went through the eight-week program he developed at the University of Massachusetts Medical Center provided him with the data to support his doctrine on how mental and emotional factors impact our physical health.[58]

Kabat-Zinn's teachings on mindfulness focus on learning to work with, rather than avoid, the stress and pain that you are experiencing. It often seems more convenient to take a pill to mask the issue than it is to be mindful of or notice what we are experiencing and let that mindfulness lead to perhaps a more sustainable solution. According to Langer, developing a mindfulness practice personally along with a mindfulness culture at work can increase productivity, innovation, leadership ability and satisfaction. It does this by keeping you in the present, which keeps you engaged.

Fredrickson reports on other research showing how mindfulness can prevent individuals from relapsing back into depression and help them to manage the stress of chronic disabilities. Like so many other methods of increasing positivity, mindfulness causes changes to brain metabolism, "reducing activity in circuits linked with negativity and increasing activity in circuits linked with positivity."[48]

Langer's research shows that most of us travel through our days in a "mindless" state, seeing the present from the perspective of the past. We are trapped in old mindsets that give the illusion that things are stable and that we know more than we do, when in fact a lot of the time we're just not paying attention to what's right in front of us. If you think of how much time you spend worrying about how something will turn out or thinking about a past conversation, you might agree with this observation.

Langer says that mindlessness is one factor that leads to burnout, lack of engagement, fatigue and conflict, all of which are common ailments of today's workplace. Burnout rates are higher in workplaces where rigid mindsets and narrow perspectives (part of what she describes as mindlessness) are more common.

Kabat-Zinn describes this as a "robot-like" way of being, and in order to change it we need to put more focus on the present moment. He defines mindfulness as "paying attention in a particular way: on purpose, in the present moment, and non-judgmentally."[59]

Mindfulness at Work

In one experiment carried out by Langer and colleagues, members of an orchestra were asked to first carry out their task as they normally would; then, they were to carry out their task mindfully and notice new things about what they were doing as they played. When the orchestra played their piece mindfully, the audience rated their enjoyment of it much higher and the orchestra members enjoyed the experience more.

Racing from task to task with a mind full of thoughts, worry and stress can be very counterproductive to our long-term goals. When I look back at most of the bad decisions I've made in my work life, they have been at times of crisis when I have not been in a mindful place.

Dr. Michael West started studying mindfulness and meditation in the seventies and did his PhD on the psychology of meditation. In my interview with him, he described the role and benefit of compassionate leadership and mindfulness to the workplace.

I increasingly feel that we have to understand as a species, as well as individuals, the interconnectedness of which we are a part—that we are connected to each other—that organizations are connected with each other—that nations are connected with each other. We are connected to our ecosystem, with other species, and with our planet.

If we are going to function collectively, we must have compassionate interconnection rather than simply competitive or hateful interconnection.

Compassion is not a touchy, feely concept. It's a very practical concept. It's about attending to the other, paying attention to one another, listening with fascination to each other. It's about understanding what they think their challenge is. It's about empathizing. It's about then taking intelligent and supportive action to help each other. If we're going to create great organizations we need more compassionate leadership. Leaders who pay attention to those they lead. Leaders who understand the situation of others. Leaders who empathize and take intelligent action to help.

But most important is attending to the other and being present. And that is where mindfulness is most important. It's not just about leaders; it's about every interaction in the organization. It's about learning to pay attention to the here and now with the other person.

That requires mindfulness. That requires practicing the ability to not get swirled away by thoughts and aspirations and anxieties and angers, but just be present with others. This is fundamental to leadership, so mindfulness plays a very important role in these interactions, but it also plays a hugely important role in all our interactions in organizational cultures.

Unfortunately, what Dr. West describes is the opposite of what we see in many organizations, where instead priorities are continually changing and people feel overwhelmed with tasks, undervalued and not truly present.

Mindfulness Practices in Action

I asked Dr. West to share an example of where mindfulness has been taught and become a regular practice in an organization. He said that there are many companies in the UK that are now using mindfulness such as the police, schools and prisons.

In the eighties and nineties, Dr. West was studying both teams in organizations and mindfulness, and he started to put the two together. He asked the question, "What happens when teams take time out on a regular basis to reflect on what they are trying to achieve and how they are going about it?"

In studying healthcare teams, they found that teams that take regular reflection time are much more productive and innovative than teams that don't. They saw these results in multiple studies, which have now been replicated by research teams in Hong Kong, Australia, Denmark, Sweden, the Netherlands and other places around the world. From Dr. West:

[Our research with healthcare teams] is an interesting example of taking mindfulness to the team level and asking teams to be

aware, to take time out, to reflect, and even to be mindful during meetings. A recent meta-analysis has shown that teams that even take 3-4 minutes at the end of meetings to review their meetings are on average 25% more effective. This is based on an analysis of 46 different studies.[60]

In my personal life, meditation and mindfulness are a part of the way I live. They are central to my work, and to the way I want to contribute in healthcare organizations. It is the water I swim in. I sit for an hour a day, every day wherever I am, at home or on a plane, and it really helps me enormously to stay grounded in the values and in the purpose of the work I do.

I asked others that I interviewed to share stories of mindfulness at work. I spoke with Melissa Barton, the Director of Organizational Development and Healthy Workplace at Sinai Health System (SHS) in Ontario, about their mindfulness initiative.

We have run six or seven mindfulness series so far, and we will now be studying the impact. It is an eight-week intensive course including a full day retreat and then six weeks where participants come together for one hour per week, followed by a full day on a weekend at the end. The approach used is recollective awareness, which is a very gentle approach to mindfulness. Rather than beating yourself up because your mind is wandering, you just keep bringing your mind back to your breath.

In this approach, Barton says you are encouraged to be gentle and curious about thoughts, stay with them and consider how you are feeling. Is it anger? Sadness? Then question why you are in that state. After reflecting, you are asked to journal about what you thought and felt.

What people find is that for the first few days you're working on this practice, you can't remember all the thoughts you had in that 20-minute silent session, so journaling is hard to do. But by the end you can slow down and find a lot of peace with it. It's something that people are gravitating to. It works well with people who are type A personalities and who beat themselves up. We are finding lots of success with this, and will be doing more research on it.

In my interview with Mary Ann Baynton, who is the Program Director of The Great-West Life Centre for Mental Health in the Workplace and the founder of Mindful Employer Canada, I asked her how mindfulness factors into shifting workplace culture. She replied:

Mindfulness is a practice of being present. There is a lot of value in the practice of mindfulness in terms of people being able to manage their emotions. Mindfulness to me is one facet of Emotional Intelligence (EI)—the ability to manage reactions and to be present in the moment so that we can also be aware of the impact that we're having on other people.

When I use the word "Mindful" in Mindful Employer, it simply means to be aware. As a manager, union rep or occupational health professional we should be asking "am I aware of the impact that I have on people and am I aware of how I am responding and reacting?" In workplaces where the leaders are stressed out under significant pressure, or feeling unsupported—it can be difficult for them to be mindful of their impact on others. I think we must start with the people in those positions and ask:

1. *are they competent to be in those positions?*
2. *are they supported to lead in a psychologically safe way?*

Dealing with emotional distress of others can be a tremendous stress on anyone. Yet, we often put people in leadership positions without the support they need to do it well.

Baynton also tells a personal story of how she used mindfulness to help make a very important decision in her life:

I had a personal decision that I needed to make about the care of my mother and I was really stressed about it. It was a very busy time and every waking moment was spent either caregiving or working. I was also worried that my stress may be having a negative effect on those around me and that I was not making good decisions about my own self-care. I decided to go away for 48 hours with no phone, no computer, no TV and no contact with anyone that I knew. I just took that time to stop. Nothing in my life changed except my perspective. It's made a huge difference. After that time of mindfully disconnecting I was able to make a good decision that had multiple positive consequences for myself, my family and my staff.

To be mindful, you just have to stop. It's not just about stopping work or going anywhere. It's about learning to take time to simply "stop frantically thinking about issues and tasks" so that you can reflect and tap into your real inner wisdom instead. We're so over-stimulated now with email, meetings, phone calls, apps, news and information that we never stop thinking. And it's not a healthy situation in or out of the workplace.

Here are some simple leadership practices to slowly integrate mindfulness into your work life:

- Langer strongly recommends encouraging play at work. She describes play as being more mindful than work and gives the example of skiing down a mountain, which is difficult to do mindlessly. When people are given permission to play they feel safe, and as a result they often will take more risks and be more creative and engaged in the process.
- Listening-based management was suggested by one of the participants in the Thoughtexchange, who said, "As managers

motivate and coordinate others in their work, they are listening to how best to advance and sustain them."

- On that note, developing mindful listening is an important leadership skill. Before you meet with someone, take a few mindful breaths and set your intention for the meeting (e.g. I intend to connect fully by listening mindfully). Be fully present, and look at the other person when they speak. Focus on what is being said versus what you are going to say next.

- Take a few minutes every so often at work to notice your bodily sensations. Is there tension anywhere? Ask, "how am I sitting or standing?" "What body language am I using?" And then consciously let go of tension.

- When you start each day, simply try to notice five new things.

- When faced with a challenge, try stopping and becoming aware of your breathing. Focus on the breath for a few moments and create space from which a mindful decision can be made. When you're ready, reflect mindfully on which direction to go.

> What leadership practices can you start today to create positive upward spirals in your team or organization?

Gratitude

One simple way to move in a positive direction is to start a gratitude practice. What I like about this practice is that it takes less than five minutes each day, but the impact can be transformational. It's as easy as getting a notebook and sitting down each morning to write down three things you are grateful for in your life. Numerous studies have shown that those who practice this habit regularly become more grateful and have higher positivity ratios.

If you're skeptical at all about this process, just try it personally for three weeks and see what happens. I once committed to keeping a gratitude journal for an entire year and observing and tracking any changes that occurred. What I noticed was as the days went on the gratitude got deeper, but I also had some very unexpected things happen.

I saw very little change in the first few weeks, but then on day 15 I had a huge shift. I completely reframed a situation and became grateful about something I had previously been feeling resentful about. On day 16 (the day after the reframing) I had the most productive day I'd had for over a year. I began picking up on things I had been procrastinating on for months. It seemed that letting go of the resentment and feeling the gratitude freed up this incredible amount of space for movement.

Others write of similar experiences, and workplaces are implementing gratitude practices with great results. A 2014 study of university employees showed increases in positive affected well-being and reduced workplace absence after a two-week intervention using gratitude. The authors comment that since this is a low cost/no cost practice that is self-guided, there is little reason not to be incorporating this type of practice into workplace initiatives.[61]

Starting a personal gratitude practice and nurturing this concept in your workplace may be one of the most impactful steps you take as a leader to improve the well-being in your organization. It is a simple, no cost/low cost practice in helping individuals to re-frame and focus on what is going right.

Gratitude Practice in Action

In my interview with Dr. Quinn, I asked him to share a story about incorporating a gratitude practice in the workplace.

The first one that comes to mind is an experience in a large business school in western United States. Kim Cameron went in one year and presented some material [on gratitude], and then they invited me the next year.

I asked who had done anything with this material? One woman who was not a faculty member put up her hand. In the University system, there are two tiers of people—there are the faculty members, who are considered the "real" people and then the others who are not faculty.

She was non-faculty and oversaw the unit. She said, "I did some research on gratitude and I started writing a journal. Then I enlisted the other people in my department to do it. We started having Thankful Thursdays where we began sharing a half-hour of gratitude." And as she said these things, the other people in her department spontaneously jumped up and started talking about how it's changed their lives, and changed their department.

Then I asked the question, "What did you feel while you were talking?" The people started answering with what they thought, and I said, "I didn't ask you what you thought, I asked you how did you feel?" I just stood there until they finally started to answer. Someone said, "It was inspiring." I said, "You realize that this is a person without a PhD. She is a staff person, and for the last five minutes she has been the leader of the business school." This is so counter to their mindset.

Gratitude as a Way of Reframing

Bad things happen. Things hit us the wrong way sometimes. Life has its own timetable. And while we may need to wallow in it awhile or have an occasional meltdown, we then have a choice.

We can invest in the bad event and the fear and get pulled into a downward spiral. Or, we can choose to reframe the event, investing in whatever piece of it we can be grateful for. The latter takes practice.

I first learned the art of reframing from past conference speaker Carla Rieger. This was during a particularly bad year where I had an uphill road to climb. The reframing process uses gratitude to replace the negative stories in our heads with positive ones. It starts with taking note of appreciations you have about yourself and your circumstances, and noticing the things that are going right in your life versus those that are not. Through a daily practice of reframing, I was able to completely change my mindset and, as a result, the project I was leading had the most financially successful year ever.

Meditation

While there are many practices that increase positivity, some have more impact than others. One of those high-impact practices is meditation, which Kabat-Zinn says is one way of getting to mindfulness. Numerous studies show that the effects of meditation tend to be cumulative, so there is a tipping point over which there are greater benefits to positivity, immunity, pain relief and more.[49,58] That tipping point is about 80-90 minutes per week. In one study, those who meditated at least this amount every week, even if they skipped a day or two, saw more benefits than those who did not.[42]

There is no right or wrong way to meditate, but many methods exist. Mindfulness-based meditation is a process of letting thoughts and feelings pass with no judgement. Kabat-Zinn developed a method of mindfulness meditation called the body scan, which has you lie on your back and focus on one body part after another, starting with one toe and eventually moving up to your head. As you focus on each area you can feel that part of your body, which moments earlier may have been outside of your awareness. This is one of the methods I find myself going back to when I meditate. He describes this in his book, "Full Catastrophe Living,"[55] but you can also search Jon Kabat-Zinn Body Scan on the internet and find numerous sources that you can download and follow.[62,63] As Mary Ann Baynton said in our interview:

The Body Scan is an easy example of how to just stop thinking, get out of your head and focus on your body. Heart Math is a very similar concept which has you imagine you are breathing through your heart. To do that you must stop thinking, because you've got to see your heart and see it expanding. The difference that makes to calm a person down can be significant. These are simple, straight-forward activities, but many people don't take the seconds to slow down and do them.

Another kind of mindfulness-based meditation is described in Barbara Frederickson's "Positivity" and is called Loving Kindness meditation. She describes this as "a technique used to increase feelings of warmth and caring for self and others." It can be done in a seated position or lying down, and starts with directing warm, loving feelings toward yourself, and then to those close to you, and then finally out to all human beings. Kabat-Zinn explains that the practice of generating feelings of empathy, compassion and love toward yourself and others has a very positive and purifying effect on your mind.

One practitioner who led us through a meditation at the conference had us count each breath as we inhaled and exhaled, going up to ten and then back down again. The idea is that if you just keep counting upwards, your mind wanders and you get caught up in thinking. Coming back down again helps you to keep your focus on your breath.

Meditation Practice in Action

Many organizations are embracing meditation as a useful practice to teach or offer space for at work. Pacific Blue Cross (PBC), for example, implemented a Meditation and Mindfulness initiative part way through a seven-year transformation happening in their organization. Wendy Quan, Manager of Change Management at PBC, implemented this initiative after seeing the stress and burnout starting to mount in the staff due to some hurdles during the first part of the transformation.[64] She began by offering weekly lunch time meditation sessions that were attended by 12 people to start. Over time she developed a "Learn to Meditate" curriculum for the workplace, which now has 26% of the workforce registered.

What PBC has found is that teaching meditation and mindfulness has helped to shift people's perceptions, attitudes and behaviours about the transformation going on at work. Among other things, the teaching includes helping people to become more self-aware of their perceptions about change, learning to mindfully choose their reactions, practicing being non-judgmental and cultivating calmness.

Employees reported learning how to manage their emotions and behaviours around the transformation, regardless of what was going on around them, while the organization observed a "calmness" throughout the transformation that has continued now that the implementation is over. A survey of participants afterward showed a 500% increase in those who reported a high ability to handle stress. Those who rated themselves as "high" on personal resilience increased by 600% after attending meditation classes, and 83% of the respondents said meditation moderately to significantly helped them through this momentous transition at work.

In her book "Thrive," Arianna Huffington writes **"...mindfulness can help us to still the noise of the world so we can listen to our inner voice."**[65] In leadership, that makes all the difference.

ACTIVITIES

Personal Practices:

1. Positivity Ratio: Go to Dr. Fredrickson's website (www. positivityresonance.com) and visit the "Tools" section to take your positivity test. Once you create an account for yourself,

which allows you to compare the results of subsequent tests, the test takes less than five minutes to do. It computes your positivity ratio over the past 24 hours. As your ratio will change from day to day, you can go back in and do this test daily or weekly and observe how the practices you are putting in place in your life impact your positivity.

If you meditate, you can also record the number of minutes each day that you meditate on this page and it will keep a log for you. This way, you can see what amount of weekly meditation affects a change to your positivity ratio.

2. Meditation: Try Jon Kabat-Zinn's body scan meditation. There are numerous recordings and videos online to lead you through this. For example, on his official site (www.mindfulnesscds.com) you can watch videos of him presenting and purchase mp3s or CD's of the mindfulness meditation series, including the body scan. I also found a few youtube videos of Kabat-Zinn leading the body scan meditation, such as this one: https://youtu.be/_DTmGtznab4.

3. Gratitude Practice: Get a small notebook or journal and start recording three things every day that you are grateful for. This could be something you do first thing when you arrive at work in the morning, or a practice you follow at home. It will take less than five minutes each day. Commit to this practice for 30 days and observe or make note of what happens.

Team Practice:

Mindful Listening: Before you lead or attend your next team meeting, set your intention to mindfully listen to others during the meeting. Share this activity with your team and ask all team

members to practice it. Here are some suggested steps you can share:
- Take a few mindful breaths before you start
- Set your intention (e.g. I intend to connect fully by listening mindfully)
- Be fully present
- Really listen when other people are speaking; look at them, and provide positive body language (lean in, nod your head, make it apparent that you are paying attention)
- Focus on what is being said, not on what you are going to say next

Organizational Practice:

Consider bringing in someone trained in teaching mindfulness and/or meditation to start an ongoing initiative that employees can participate in. Create a private, quiet place where employees can go to meditate or take some reflection time amidst their day.

Featured Influencer: Mary Ann Baynton

Mary Ann Baynton

Mary Ann's area of focus is workplace mental health. She is author and co-author of several books such as "Mindful Manager, Keeping Well at Work, Preventing Workplace Meltdown, Building Stronger Teams" and "Resolving Workplace Issues."

In her latest book, "The Evolution of Workplace Mental Health in Canada: Toward a standard for psychological health and safety," Mary Ann draws on her experience as a chair of the committee responsible for the development of the National Standard of Canada on Psychological Health and Safety in the Workplace. A world first, this voluntary standard helps employers prevent psychological harm to employees.

Mary Ann has served as the Program Director for the Great-West Life Centre for Mental Health in the Workplace for over a decade. The Centre helps all employers, not just its clients, address psychological health and safety in their workplaces. The Centre hosts roundtables to discuss issues, supports new research, and partners with experts in the creation of new resources. These resources are provided free of charge to everyone to help with the prevention, intervention and management of workplace mental health issues.

Mary Ann was awarded the Canadian Workplace Wellness Pioneer Award in 2013. Her mission is to improve working lives by facilitating work relationships and environments where all can flourish.

To view her publications and services, go to: www.maryannbaynton.com.

FLOURISH

Teams

POSITIVELY DEVIANT

A) First core team: Jeanie (Cloutier), Muneerah (Kassam), Deb (Connors) & Sheron (Stone), 1997
B) First team retreat 2003: Deb, Jonathan, Alison, Muneerah, Dal, Andrea (Mau)
C) Fun team activity at Conference 2011
D) Conference 2000 on-site team: David, Dal, Muneerah, Deb, John, Lesley, Andrea (McDonald), Robin
E) Trudy Boyle, Martin Collis, Conference 2006

FUN

INFLUENCE
Emergent Process

COMMUNITY

A) Fun & games at Conference 2002
B) Hiking at Lake Louise Conference 2002
C) Yay! A better place to work!
D) Workplace health really can be this much fun!
E) Celebrating –Kelly Blackshaw, Monica Kohlhammer, Kendy Bentley
F) Making connections, Conference 2012

140

A) Greeters at Conference 2001 in Calgary. (It was a family affair: Deb's Mom, Dad, Sister-in-law, and Uncle are in this picture!)
B) 10th Birthday Celebration: Conference 2006
C) "...and we'll take on leading the conference." (Deb & Munerah's girls - they came with us!)
D) A community celebrating the end of an era, Conference 2013
E) David Gouthro (with nose flute), Annie and Linda Duxbury, 2002

Shift
Yourself
1st

A

Awards

B

C

E

UPSTREAM
Vision
SHIFT YOURSELF 1ST

D

A) 1998 debate: Don Ardell & Ron Labonte with referee Kendy!
B) Martin and Mary Ann: so much to share!
C) We were all about changing the world
D) Warren Redman, speaker & Francois Lagarde, moderator, Conference 2008
E) Craig Thompson and Kendy Bentley giving pioneer award to Ian Arnold, Conference 2012

CHAPTER 7

"A positive people culture is one where people experience positive emotions, optimism, cohesion, gratitude and humour, and where they consequently have a real sense of engagement"
—**Dr. Michael West, Europe's leading expert on healthcare leadership**

What if we took all the practices that have been introduced up to this point in the book and applied them to our most immediate team, implementing them into the way we operated? As West told us in Chapter Three, by applying all the principles from their research to their teams at the Aston Business School, they were able achieve the best staff morale of any academic institution in Britain.

In our interview, West said, "It is a well-established finding from the research that we need to create environments that are positive for people to work in." You might be thinking that this is painfully obvious, but West says that in most organizations, teamwork is not well developed. What is the situation in your workplace?

Positive and resilient teams improve organizational performance. In part, this is due to improving the well-being of the individual team members. Effective teams significantly increase their members' resilience through reducing stress, improving well-being, and providing support.[66]

Dr. Michael West has studied team and organizational innovation and effectiveness for many decades, and is the author of over 200 scholarly articles and 20 books on the subject. He teaches organizations solutions to become more effective and innovative.

West and others from the University of Lancaster set up another company in 2003, called AstonOD, with the sole purpose of developing more positive and resilient teams in healthcare. They have now worked with over 100 healthcare organizations, focusing on coaching individual teams as well as teaching "inter-team working," which means teams working well with other teams. Their work over the years with the National Health Service (NHS) in the UK has shown overwhelming evidence that increasing positivity and resilience in teams and organizations is possible, and that this has tremendous impact on organizational performance. When asked what practices they used, West said:

> *We focused on developing skills through coaching teams within these organizations to make sure that they have a clear, inspiring purpose, clear objectives and clear roles. Also, making sure they meet regularly and that meetings are positive.*
>
> *It is important that leaders understand their role and how important building positivity and resilience in their teams is. We taught leaders how to listen to all the diverse voices and to create shared leadership, and in particular how to work across team boundaries so that different teams work together effectively.*

I was astonished to hear from West that with only a 5% increase in staff working in positive, resilient teams, they observed a 3.3% decline in patient mortality! For the average hospital in the UK, that is a reduction of 40 deaths per year. This is attributed to lower levels of errors, stress and accidents. West's team determined that a 25% decrease in the number of health service staff working in negative and non-resilient teams would save 5000 lives every year, which is a conservative estimate.

Much of the research on effective teamwork supports using many of the practices we've covered in this book already, such as:

- Asking transformational questions (e.g. What is our purpose?)
- Appreciative inquiry (e.g. Who are we as a team, when we are at our best?)
- Engaging team members in change processes
- Rewarding the behaviours we want to see
- Having authentic conversations
- Increasing positive emotion through gratitude and mindfulness practices

This next section describes additional leadership practices that can be applied at the team level, and examples of how to integrate them into your culture at work.

Do you have Real Teams or Pseudo Teams in Your Workplace?

A group of people is not a "team," says Dr. West. Neither is a hierarchy. In an annual survey of employees of the NHS, the question "do you work in a team?" is asked, and 90% typically answer yes. However, when asked three further questions that determine whether the team is a "real" team or a "pseudo" team, that number drops to 40%. The questions asked are:

1. Does your team have clear objectives?
2. Do you work closely together to achieve those objectives?
3. Do you meet regularly to review your performance and how it can be improved?

Based on these questions, would you say that your team is real or pseudo? If you are on a real team, consider your current state before reading on. Are your meetings positive? Are you building team practices to support resilience? What ideas can you draw from the previous chapters to increase the positivity of your team meetings?

> What can your organization do to enhance team performance?

Develop a Set of Team Practices

In my interview with Dr. Martin Shain, he suggests that every team develop a set of practices.

> *The typical problem I see with teams is the growing perception of inequity within the team or perceived unfairness. In the Neighbour at Work Initiative we developed, we provide a way to surface that type of thinking, address how we affect each other and learn more about each other's basic needs.*[67]
>
> *Learning that your work colleague has small children at home, for example, or has an elderly father in an assisted living facility may help you to understand why they don't stay late at work, or are unable to take on more on a project.*
>
> *The idea is that by developing a set of agreed upon practices, they will become normative after a certain period.*

When developing a set of practices, West suggests that some of the practices to consider are those that allow for clarity around team membership, size and purpose, as well as having challenging objectives.

Team Reflexivity

Taking time to reflect on how effective your team is and adapting new practices to improve your team is called Team Reflexivity. West breaks this down into the two key elements required for effective teams: task reflexivity, which covers how effective the team is at achieving its objectives, and social reflexivity, which includes how the team supports the well-being of its members, both socially and emotionally.[66,68]

Lots of teams are very task effective. But if they do not have a good socio-emotional climate they will only succeed in the short term, and eventually they will break down. A resilient team requires both elements.

The remaining leadership practices in this chapter focus on the social reflexivity of teams—creating the social and emotional climate for teams to succeed. Social reflexivity requires transformational leadership, high levels of positive emotion in the team, and continual renewal.

Improving Social Reflexivity Through Positivity

Part of improving social reflexivity is to find ways to increase positivity in your team. As West says,

> *The important thing is that we have a very strong balance of positive to negative emotions. We can debate whether the best ratio is 3:1 or 5:1—but the point is we must create environments that are positive for people.*

As his research in healthcare organizations has shown, when the team supports the well-being of its members, the climate becomes more positive. West has said, "I have yet to see convincing data that too much positivity is a problem!"

At AstonOD, a variety of assessments have been developed to measure positivity and resilience in teams. These are validated measures that have been used in their research over the years. A brief one-page team positivity test called the Aston Team Positivity Measure is included in the Resources section in this book. It will give you a baseline idea of where your team is at in terms of positive and negative emotion.

Try adding some of the ideas to your team practices, such as mindful listening from Chapter Six, or using some of the suggestions from the Aston Team Positivity Measure such as encouraging the use of positive language and celebrating team achievements. Once these practices have become consistent, conduct the team positivity test again to see how it has changed.

Team Debriefs

As mentioned in Chapter Six, a recent meta-analysis of 46 different studies on the impact of debriefs showed that those teams who regularly carry out this practice are on average 25% more effective.[69]

A team debrief is a review of a meeting, project or training that uses reflection, discussion, self-discovery and goal setting to learn from each situation. The researchers recommend that debriefs be a part of all team trainings and meetings as a focus on how to continually improve. Guidelines drawn from the meta-analysis include assuring that the debrief:

- Is **active** (all team members are involved in providing feedback) versus passive (one person is providing feedback and the group is listening)
- Is **developmental** (used to discuss and develop new and better ways of being as a team) versus punitive (used to punish)
- Is **specific** (examining a specific event or meeting versus a general examination of team practices)
- Uses **multiple** sources (e.g. gathers feedback from observers outside the team in addition to team members)
- Is **facilitated**, preferably by an impartial source. Studies showed that facilitated debriefs seem to be more effective due to the ability of these facilitators to introduce new questions, draw out

ideas from all team members and provide some structure and focus that the team leader sometimes cannot.

Overall, team debriefs can be a relatively easy but very powerful and low cost way to increase team performance.

Empowering People

Dr. Graham Lowe reports that one of the big themes he has seen in his work with the Quality Workplace Awards through the Ontario Hospital Association is empowerment.

When you have front line groups such as patient care or housekeeping who are empowered and, in some cases, empower themselves to find better ways of delivering their service, that engagement process and sense of ownership they have over what they can do and how they can contribute to the big goals sets the stage perfectly for teams to grab onto problems and find solutions.

There are endless examples across the provinces of employees making the process of care delivery more efficient, finding new models, and examining the way they work as a team. It's the process of empowering front-line people to do a better job, and trusting them to figure out how they can do it.

Some organizations use methods like suggestion boxes and provide prizes and incentives to employees who come up with new, more effective ways of working or better ways to provide customer service. In what ways can you further empower your employees to come up with new ideas and suggestions to improve teamwork and productivity?

Emotional Intelligence

One way that teams and organizations can build resilience, according to Emotional Intelligence expert Marie Mac Donald, is through incorporating daily EI practices. EI is the ability to recognize, understand and manage our own emotions as well as the emotions of others.[70]

Mac Donald coaches executives on EI skills. She runs a Human Resources Development company that works with organizations to support positive culture shift. In our interview, I asked her how EI helps create more positive teams and organizations.

Because Emotional Intelligence skills help people to become more aware of themselves and of how they impact others, it allows more integrity and more authenticity, and it allows people to see where they need to do some work.

One of the things I think is absolutely central to improving our EI is to have a learning mindset—to be open to learning, to be open to growing and developing. Not to think you're already done, but to see yourself as a "work in progress." I've been working on this for 40 years, and I'm still working on it all the time myself in conversations with clients, or even in conversations with my family. I'm trying to manage "me" while I am showing up in a relationship. It's ongoing work.

I may not be noticing if people are angry or upset and they're not on board if I don't have that deep awareness and mindfulness. I highly recommend that leaders get EI profiled. It allows them to get a real-time measure of who they are and how they show up.

The other part of EI is to be open to feedback—to set the stage to get feedback from others, and to act on that feedback. Everybody needs to be doing this. For example, asking, "How am I impacting you right now? I notice that you stopped talking. Did I come on too strong?" Good organizations and leaders do this all the time.

West agrees that self-awareness is the most important element of EI and suggests that leaders train for self-awareness much like an athlete trains for their sport. One suggestion he makes is to catch yourself ten times each day and note how you are feeling. This is a way of practicing mindfulness. Keeping a diary of when you feel emotionally positive or negative (and why) is another suggestion. Look for patterns in the flow of your feelings so that you can determine what triggers them.

Hiring

Workplace health expert Mary-Lou MacDonald stresses that creating a positive team environment starts with hiring the right people.

> *You can create positive cultures within unhealthy organizations by focusing on who is in your circle of influence. It's about getting the right people on the bus, both from a skill perspective and a culture perspective. Include the rest of the team when you're interviewing for someone new. Aside from skills, look at "do they fit in terms of personality and sense of humour?"*

I was once hired in this way for a management position. The interviewers were the three people who would end up directly reporting to me, and it was their recommendation to the director that got me hired. I liked the process so much, we used it the next time we hired someone for this team. The whole team was a part of the interviewing process, and we added a set of objective criteria where we gave points for each aspect of "fit" within our culture in addition to task requirements of the job.

For one interview, I remember how important it was to have that objective criteria grid. There were four of us on the interview panel. We all subjectively felt that one candidate would be best for the job. When we added up the points we gave each candidate for each of the objective criteria though, someone else came up on top because of her cultural fit. We went with the objective decision and it turned out that this candidate was ideal for the team, enhanced our team in many ways and stayed with us for years.

Dealing with Team Conflict

Mary Ann Baynton told me a story of how a practice she uses worked with one of her clients:

> *In one case where I used this practice there had been several complaints in this team, and many were off on stress leave because of the situation while others were looking at changing jobs. What was interesting was that there were other people who didn't even know there was anything wrong. When I interviewed each person individually I found many different perspectives. This helps you to understand that perception IS reality, and unless we create a shared perception of the behaviours that are acceptable, we're always going to have those different perspectives. The way to go forward in a workplace like this isn't to pull out a "respect in the workplace" policy and say this is what we must do, because most people feel they haven't violated anything and yet the respect and civility isn't there.*
>
> *Some people will be more vulnerable to teasing, to abruptness, to being excluded than others will be. And we must understand that is just a part of the human condition and part of any diversity in a group. So, the process that I use is to interview each of these people individually and privately and I ask them a set of questions.*

Mary Ann starts her process of creating a shared set of expectations and behaviours by asking each person on the team this set of questions:
1. What is already good about this place that you wouldn't want to lose if there were to be some changes?

2. What would need to change for you to be excited about coming to work, supported to do a good job, and able to leave with energy at the end of the day?

3. What would you be willing to do differently to reach your goal in the question above?

4. If, for some reason, you were having a bad day and not following the shared expectations that will be developed from these interviews, how would you want others to approach you about it or what do you believe would be a reasonable consequence?

If you consider these questions, you will recognize practices we have discussed in past chapters in each of them:

- Question 1 incorporates the practice of gratitude, asking about "what is good?"
- Question 2 incorporates the practice from positive organizing of "seeing the possibilities."
- Question 3 uses the practice we discussed in Chapter Three of asking "how can I be a contribution?"
- Question 4 applies the practice of creating shared vision and developing the practices to achieve it.

Putting together the answers from all the people she has interviewed, Mary Ann looks for themes and patterns. She says that each time, the solution is as unique as the group of people. She develops a set of shared expectations and behaviours that have come directly from the people themselves.

If one person says something and no one else does, it's not going to be in the final agreement. But where most the people agree that something should be a certain way, we put it together, and I ask them all if they are willing to work under and sign on to this approach. The reason this works is because there is not an expert coming in telling people what to do. That rarely works. It is not a cookie-cutter approach. People feel they have been heard, and there is no shame. It's not looking at who is right and who is wrong like an investigation. The investigation is always just a matter of perspectives anyway, and it rarely ends up with people feeling good about working with each other. So, instead, we simply say "how do we want to work together going forward?" The agreement belongs to the people in the group, and we also have a plan if someone isn't willing to follow the guidelines. We can hold them accountable. These plans become something by the group, for the group.

With the team from the earlier story, Mary Ann said that changes happened the minute she read the report to the group.

It's almost immediate because, no one feels blamed or shamed. Therefore no one has a need to react defensively. It's not enough to create the agreement though. It is only sustainable if the leader in charge holds everyone, including themselves, accountable in the way the agreement suggests, and this must be from day one.

In this group, what was interesting was that the employees who were most upset almost always blamed the manager. And yet, when we talked about what needed to be different, it ended up being more about how the team members interacted with each other. Often people blame the manager when there is disrespect and incivility among the team members.

In the process I use, the document doesn't blame anyone. So, the manager wasn't singled out. But my advice to any leader where there is a very dysfunctional team is that the leader needs to take responsibility for the team dysfunction. It doesn't mean they need to take the blame, because maybe they didn't cause it. Taking the blame is much different than taking responsibility. Taking responsibility says, "I'm really sorry things are this way. I want to change things and I'm willing to take responsibility to help enact that change and sustain it." It helps people to refocus, as opposed to when a leader is defensive and wants to find out whose fault it is.

Another interesting observation Mary Ann made about this process is that in the end, when she reads the report back to them, most people think "that's my story; that's what I wanted." She says that it is very common, even in a dysfunctional team, that all members share the same specific approaches to a great working environment. They just needed some help to discover this.

Thoughtexchange Ideas

Teamwork was a topic of discussion in our Thoughtexchange. As one respondent put it:

It's human nature to want to belong. When we foster inclusive and positive team spirit, employees look forward to coming to work. Teams that help each other out when things get crazy or support each other's work are much more productive than those employees who feel alone and unsupported.

When asked "What practices have you experienced (or heard of) that have improved team culture," the suggested practices from the Thoughtexchange included:

Role Clarity:
- "Acknowledging the role of everyone on the team and the importance of what they do creates a positive energy to keep everyone rowing in the same direction."

Look at Effective Teams Elsewhere:
- "Identification of bright spots. Look at teams that report a positive work culture and explore them."

Team Charters:
- "Team charter processes that are measured and tracked for compliance can be very effective."

Share the Team Chair Role:
- "In a team I was in, a different employee became the meeting facilitator employee each month. It truly empowered the notion that everyone was equal in the organization. You felt it!"

Recognition:
- "Message boards. In lunchrooms set up a white board where employees can write brief stories about other teammates that went above and beyond the call of duty to help other team mates."
- "We use an employee recognition program to have people submit written nominations of other staff for awards for demonstrating specific leadership behaviours in the workplace. The nominations are announced publicly at staff meetings."

Reflection:
- "Teams getting together to talk about their culture and how to improve. Often, we don't get together to discuss this because we're too busy doing our jobs. Once we understand (through measurement) where we're currently at, we can identify areas to work on. This can become a shared focus for the entire team."

Team Building:
- "Team building. In one place I worked, teams would take three to four day team building adventures off-site."
- "Cook together. There's no stronger connection than the one we have over food. Events where teams chop and sauté together forge lasting connections."
- "Seasonal lunches out together as a team. Try to walk there together. Everyone is invited."
- "Treats and team meetings. People can take turns bringing them. Celebrate team member's birthdays with cake."
- "In one team, we used to make Friday lunches a team affair. It helped the team to relax and ponder on their week's successes."

What ideas from this Thoughtexchange interest you? How can you tailor them to use within your teams?

Practices in Action

Mersey Care is one example of a NHS organization that has seen encouraging results through working toward more positive and resilient teams. They are a mental healthcare organization in the North West of England and have worked with AstonOD to learn about and implement team-based learning.

They initially sent 33 clinicians and support staff from their 32 worksites to be trained as coaches. Then all team leaders throughout the organization were provided with tool kits of practices to use with their teams, and the newly trained coaches were available to assist.

Dr. West states that they have seen astonishing results in care-quality, patient satisfaction and staff well-being. Improvements have been made in all measures of the employee experience (such as role clarity and feeling valued) and patient satisfaction (such as patients feeling supported and involved in decision-making).[71]

Graham Lowe provides another example of team-based practices in action in this story he shared from Royal Victoria Regional Health Centre in Barrie, Ontario. He says,

> *In hospitals, it is not pay that differentiates—it is the work that becomes the competitive advantage in recruiting. At Royal Victoria Regional Health Centre they started doing the "Viccie" Awards where they asked teams to submit short videos to show how the team lives the values of the hospital through their work, and in particular how they care for patients. The videos show the high level of engagement that these employees have because they do it themselves. They really signify what the values mean to the employees in different parts of the organization, and it becomes a very powerful way of defining the hospitals brand as an employer.*

What are your current team practices like? Do you have mostly real teams or pseudo teams? What improvements would your organization see if you could increase positivity and resilience in your teams by 5%, like NHS did? Try implementing the practices below to get started on your journey toward team improvement.

ACTIVITIES

Personal Practices:

1. This is a personal practice for you as a team leader. Ask these questions of yourself, with your team in mind, and then ask them of your team at the next team meeting you are facilitating:
   - Do we have a real team?
   - What is our purpose?
   - Is the purpose clear and inspiring?
   - Is our team the right size?

- Do we have clear objectives?
- Do people understand their roles?

2. Start a diary to make notes about your positive and negative emotions throughout the day (or add this to your leadership journal). Catch yourself ten times each day and note how you are feeling. Look for patterns and triggers to help you become more self-aware.

3. Reflect on what ideas from this chapter you can add to your through-line. Are these a part of your next three turns? Your "this week" or "this month" goals? Your "someday" plans? Wherever they best fit, make sure to capture these ideas for future.

Team Practices:

Conduct the AstonOD Team Positivity Measure, included in the Resources section, to get a baseline idea of where your team is in terms of positive and negative emotion. Discuss the results as a team, and determine ways in which you can increase team positivity. Consider these questions as a starting point:
- What set of practices can we develop to improve positivity and resilience in our team?
- How can we improve our social reflexivity?
- Are our meetings positive?
- What can we do to increase the positivity of our meetings?

Consider adopting and tailoring some of the practices discussed in this chapter (and previous chapters) to work with your team, such as:
- Starting meetings with a round of gratitude
- Practicing mindful listening
- Encouraging positive language

- Celebrating team achievements
- Developing a team vision board in your meeting space
- Using a team conflict process like the one Mary Ann Baynton shared to move forward when conflict arises
- Adding a team debrief to the end of each meeting
- Reviewing the ideas from the Thoughtexchange discussion and tailoring these to meet the needs of your team

Conduct the AstonOD Team Positivity Measure every 6-12 months as you begin to adopt new practices to see how this impacts the positive emotions of your team.

Organizational Practice:

To improve teamwork throughout your organization, consider these questions and the practices that can be developed from a company-wide perspective:

- What consistent practices can be incorporated throughout all teams in your organization to foster positivity and continual renewal?
- Is there a toolkit you could develop for each team leader to give them ideas and support for working with their teams?
- How does scheduling on projects allow for, or take away from, continual renewal? How can scheduling be changed on an organizational level with continual renewal in mind?
- What coaching can be provided to your team leaders to help provide team leadership that is consistently positive?
- What team retreats can be planned on a consistent basis to allow for continual renewal and reflection as an organization?

Featured Influencer: Dr. Michael West

Professor Michael A. West

Michael West is Head of Thought Leadership at the King's Fund, London and Professor of Organizational Psychology at Lancaster University Management School. He has authored, edited or co-edited 20 books and has published over 200 articles for scientific and practitioner publications.

The focus of his research over 30 years has been culture and leadership in organizations, team and organizational innovation and effectiveness, particularly in relation to the organization of health services. He provides regular policy advice to many UK National Health Service organizations.

He led the Department of Health Policy Research Programme into cultures of quality and safety in the NHS in England from 2009 to 2013. He also led the NHS National Staff Survey development and implementation for eight years. He assisted Health Education England and NHS Improvement in developing the national framework on improvement and leadership development in England ("Developing People, Improving Care," 2016) and the Department of Health in Northern Ireland in developing the Collective Leadership Strategy for Health and Social Care (2017).

Dr. West also provided substantial input to the development of NHS England's culture and collective leadership programme, now being employed by many health care organizations. He lectures widely both nationally and internationally about compassionate leadership for health services and the results of his research and solutions for developing effective and innovative health care organizations.

For more on West's research see http://www.lancaster.ac.uk/lums/people/michael-west.

CHAPTER 8

Inspire Psychological Health

"What happens in the workplace doesn't stay in the workplace. It migrates out to families and communities and society at large as net social capital or net social loss."

—Dr. Martin Shain, Principal, Neighbour at Work

Creating a psychologically safe and healthy work environment is not something we do well.

Most employers are getting better at understanding how to recognize, address and accommodate for mental *illness*, but we're not adept at inspiring mental *wellness*. In fact, countless work situations do the opposite. They cause psychological damage in the form of excessive stress, burnout, sleep disorders, anxiety and fear.[72,73,74] Obviously, these conditions do not lead to flourishing and are detrimental to personal and organizational success.

Like all other aspects of creating a better place to work, it is the daily practices we participate in that will improve the psychological and emotional climate over time. All the practices discussed thus far in the book contribute to a more positive psychological climate, particularly the practices that improve positive emotions like gratitude, mindfulness and meditation as well as the principles of positive organizing.

Encouraging our workforce to develop resilient cycles in order to replace vicious ones contributes to positive psychological health, as do the practices of reflective action and examining our hypocrisies as leaders. All of these need to be practiced regularly.

This chapter provides further stories of how organizations have inspired psychological health and well-being at work, along with leadership practices that can help you to create the foundation from which to build psychological health within your workplace.

First, Do No Harm

The promise to "First, Do No Harm," a principle of bioethics taught to every healthcare practitioner in his or her training, would go a long way if applied as a principle in every workplace. At a minimum, let us not send people home from work more broken and less psychologically and physically healthy than when they entered it. But what if we took this step further and we made employees' overall well-being the primary consideration when making business decisions?

Following the "First, Do No Harm" principle makes good business sense. Research has shown that organizations with a positive approach to psychological health and safety at work perform better, have more success in recruitment and retention, and achieve higher engagement, better productivity, and more creativity and innovation.[75]

Thanks to some key individuals and organizations, awareness of psychological health at work in Canada has increased, and ideas are shifting upstream to the creation of work cultures that support positive mental health.

There is a myriad of new tools available, including the National Standard of Canada for Psychological Health & Safety in the Workplace (the "Standard"), a voluntary set of guidelines, tools and resources focused on promoting employees' mental health and preventing psychological harm due to workplace factors. It was championed by the Mental Health Commission of Canada and developed by the Canadian Standards Association. Canada is the first country in the world to develop a Standard for Psychological Health & Safety in the workplace.[76]

What is intimated in the Standard but not commonly understood is the notion of how to build a culture that promotes positive mental wellness for everyone, and how a leader's practices impact this. One organization that is leading the way in embracing the vision of positive mental health for all, and taking employee well-being into account in their decision making, is Sinai Health System.

Sinai Health System's Story

Melissa Barton has been a proponent of workplace health for decades and spoke at some of our early conferences. She is now Director of Organizational Development & Healthy Workplace at Sinai Health System in Toronto.

Sinai Health System, comprised of Mount Sinai Hospital, Bridgepoint Active Healthcare, Circle of Care and Lunenfield-Tanenbaum Research Institute, is one of the early adopters of the Standard, which Barton lists as one of her most highly recommended tools.

There is a risk assessment part of the Standard, which is a short set of questions called the "Initial Scan" that computes a Stress Satisfaction Offset Score (SSOS) and the Stress Satisfaction Index (SSIX). The questions are used to start conversations about the balance between effort, reward, demand and control. In other words, does the satisfaction people get from their work offset the stress they have?

Decades of research show that the situation of having high demand (having too many demands over a long a period with constant imposed deadlines) combined with low control (having little influence over decisions that affect you) creates strain, which may lead to injury, disease, depression or other illnesses. Similarly, too much mental or physical effort coupled with too little compensation or acknowledgement is associated with increased cardiovascular disease and mental health issues.[77] When the balance changes to increase employee control in these situations (e.g. I still have many demands, but I now have the control to deal with them), stress decreases. The SSIX adds two more questions to the mix to assess perceived fairness and support from supervisors, because these factors mediate the impact of stress in the workplace.

Sinai Health System embedded these psychological safety principles into a people change model used to help them through a merger. From Barton:

> *We are working with managers to make sure they are thinking about which employees on their teams may be more vulnerable. What are some of the strategies they need to put in place as they go through change to make sure their psychological safety is considered? As they are restructuring jobs, are they looking at the balance between effort/reward and demand/control?*
>
> *Our focus is to embed psychological safety into all our change processes. We are using Psychological Safety Risk Assessment tools and then taking steps to help relieve stress. We are helping people learn how to do reflective practices for themselves.*

For example, some reflective questions they suggest their employees ask themselves are:
- How am I reacting to the change?
- What is my emotional state like?
- Where am I in the change process?
- How, then, am I going to be able to lead my team in a way that is healthy?

They are also insuring that their disability management program includes psychological health:

Part of our Healthy Workplace System is making sure that our disability management programs take the same approach with psychological disabilities as they do with physical disabilities. For example, if we're returning someone to work with a mental disability we want to take the approach we do when it is a physical one, which means if they're not back to 100%, that doesn't mean they can't come back to work. They can have a gradual return to work. We don't want to exclude people from the working environment, because we know that the longer people are way, the harder it is to come back.

Sinai Health System is unique in how they came to see the importance of psychological health and safety at work. When I interviewed Barton, she told me the story of how this happened.

Our journey to focus on Emotional Well-Being came about through the SARS Epidemic. Mount Sinai Hospital was one of the hospitals that treated SARS patients at the time of the outbreak in 2003. Employees still talk of how they were stigmatized in the community because of fears that they were exposed to the disease and may be contagious, and how traumatic that was to them.

It was during this time that our Department of Psychiatry developed a strategy to support their colleagues. They talked about how important it was to support staff while maintaining our patient focus. As a result, they initiated the Emotional Well-Being Team to build evidence-based healthy practices for employees. This team includes clinicians and leaders from the departments of Psychiatry, Human Resources, Organizational Development, Nursing, Human Rights and Health Equity.

Sinai Health System's long-standing Emotional Well-Being initiative has the mission "to lead efforts that eliminate health inequity." Barton said that this is part of their heritage, as their hospital was originally built in 1923 to provide services to the Jewish immigrant population when there was a lot of discrimination against them. She says, "When we talk about being true to our heritage at Mount Sinai, it's about making sure that we're offering programs and services for people who are marginalized."

One group that can be marginalized is people with mental health issues and addictions, which is why Sinai Health System adopted the Standard along with other initiatives that promote positive psychological health. There are 3 pillars to their Emotional Well-Being Initiative:

- **Employee Health Resources** (programs aimed at improving individual resiliency, coping and well-being)
- **Healthy Culture** (initiatives aimed at building a culture of support, caring and carefulness), and
- **Healthy Workplace Systems** (such as the Standard and inter-professional committees)

Finding ways to recognize and reward balance, fairness and community within our organizations is one way leaders can inspire psychological well-being. A feature program that Sinai Health System offers to promote positive psychological health is called "Are you an ALLY?" It is a campaign that teaches people how to be an ally to one another. Barton explains:

We formed a committee called "The Committee for Ending Discrimination Against People with Mental Health Issues." The committee includes staff and patient members, and together we developed the Ally Campaign materials. We now have posters and videos around the hospital raising awareness around avoiding language like "crazy," "nuts" or "druggies" and to check in and support colleagues and friends who may have mental health and addictions issues.

Sinai Health also developed a learning package to support the "Are You an ALLY?" campaign for other marginalized groups as well. The focus is on learning to be an ally for any person who is being discriminated against so that they do not feel like they are in a psychologically unsafe situation. It teaches people to interrupt discrimination or harassment when it occurs.

Through the campaign, they teach many reflective practices and use tools such as a "privilege" checklist that helps people to reflect on situations they may not have thought about, but that may be offensive. Barton says that from a cultural perspective it is interesting to see people start changing their language.

> *At the start, people were saying, "Seriously, I can't use the word crazy even to describe my day?" And we would say, "Can't you use a different word other than crazy? Why don't you use busy, or be more specific? You can come up with a word that's not going to offend, right?"*
>
> *So, it's interesting to watch how people check their language and each other's language now, and keep working at it. It's part of a learning culture to realize that "when I said that, it would have offended someone. I have to do some learning there." It causes people to be more reflective about their language.*

Barton's story demonstrates that certain practices, when used consistently, can make a difference to workplace culture. The practices used at Sinai Health System that have shown successful results have included:

- Getting organizational conversations going about the balance between stress and satisfaction by using the SSOS, first as a measurement tool and then to start the conversations.
- Embedding psychological health and safety into all workplace change processes.

- Leaders using reflective practices, and then teaching these practices to others in the workplace.
- Working toward eliminating health inequity (making sure that people with psychological health issues are not marginalized).
- Developing communication campaigns that get conversations going about psychological health at work.
- Changing language that is offensive.

As Barton says, "Our greatest resources are our staff members, and investing in their well-being contributes to patient care."

Setting a Foundation for Psychological Wellness

Sinai Health System has developed many practices that have set a strong foundation for psychological wellness within their organization. I asked the other experts I interviewed the question, "What can leaders do differently to set a foundation for psychological health in the workplace?" The advice they shared falls into these five main categories that are further explained below:

- Making psychological health a part of the workplace conversation.
- Declaring your vision and commitment to transform culture.
- Maximizing mental energy.
- Developing psychological contracts.
- Measuring the balance between stress and satisfaction in your organization.

Make Psychological Health a Part of the Workplace Conversation

Dr. Martin Shain, whose background research was instrumental in bringing forward the Standard, says that the biggest single change he has seen in the past decade is that people are talking about psychological health more. He teaches a class at York University on Psychological Health and Safety, where the students are from workplaces that are struggling with how to deal with psychological health at work.

Many of them say that although we may not be as far along as we would like, at least it has now become part of the language in meetings, collective bargaining, and HR policies. As Shain says,

> *Psychological safety and how we achieve it is being used as a criterion for evaluating the merit of other types of initiatives and policies. For example, if we're going to change our recruitment policy, we are starting to ask how attentive it is to the need to recruit people who are going to be emotionally intelligent in the way they deal with people.*
>
> *When we talk about changing our promotion or advancement policies, we are asking how much we take psychological health into account. The permeation of the language and ideas about psychological safety through the various touch points of the employment relationship, from recruitment and hiring; to training, orientation and promotion; to discipline and dismissal is what I'm seeing.*
>
> *I like to think that we're seeing the very early signs of an evolution within the employment relationship. The signs are fairly weak but distinct.*

Shain's earlier work revolved around the idea that there is a single super-duty of care to provide a psychologically safe system of work. It is not regulated by law, but is intimated in so many different decisions in the law.

Paying attention to this super-duty of care will save employers from grievances, Workers' Compensation claims, law suits, human rights claims and vast amounts of long- and short-term disability claims.

Corporate lawyers have come to understand that this is good advice. "You do this one thing and you will be steering the course that gets you above most of the bad weather. That was the origin of the Standard," says Shain.

Declare Your Vision and Commitment to Transform Culture

Shain stresses that for culture to shift and for tools like the Standard to make a difference, it is imperative that leaders be vocal about their vision and commitment to transforming the culture.

> *When people talk about the Standard, most just talk about the management system part of it.*
>
> *I think the governance philosophy needs to be pulled out as a key starting point. Leaders need to declare their vision of how the workplace should be run based on the recognition that how we relate to each other in the workplace affects our mental health in significant ways. They need to make a commitment to a "careful workplace" (avoidance of reasonably foreseeable harm) in which every effort is made to prevent negligent, reckless and intentional harm to the mental health of workers. That's the vision of the Standard.*
>
> *The key part is leaders acknowledging that conduct in the workplace affects mental health, and that we can shape that conduct in more positive ways. They must set the compass and direct the organization along that road.*
>
> *Often when the Standard is used, leaders give a weak message. It has got to be more of a living commitment. The proof of commitment is the assignment of appropriate resources.*
>
> *The Standard, when taken seriously, is a transformational vehicle. It is meant to encourage the transformation of how we*

behave toward one another in the workplace to achieve a higher level of mental health. And not just in the workplace—the original Standard as proposed was a population health initiative.

Maximize Mental Energy

When asked about what the most significant changes have been regarding psychological health in the workplace, Mary Ann Baynton from the Great-West Life Centre for Mental Health in the Workplace sees that leaders are recognizing the connection between mental health and performance.

She says leaders are now more aware that the measures they talk about—such as performance management, organizational culture, engagement, work-life balance, innovation and creativity—are all built upon the mental health, mental well-being and mental energy of employees.

When we talk about workplace mental health, we are not talking about people with depression. We are talking about the mental energy of your employees to do their best work. It is a really good business tactic to maximize mental energy.

> What can you do today to start a shift toward maximizing mental energy for all in your workplace?

Develop Psychological Contracts

Dr. Linda Duxbury recommends that managers go through psychological contract exercises with their employees on a regular basis. A psychological contract is what we believe or perceive about the informal obligations between an employer and employee, and is not necessarily written in the legal employment contract.[78] As Duxbury says,

> *Every employee has a legal contract including pay, benefits, vacation, and job title. But there are a lot of unwritten, unstated expectations on both the part of the employee and the employer. One of the most damaging things that can happen is called psychological contract violation. For example, you think that if you come in and work hard, and you're loyal and dedicated, your job is safe and you'll be protected. You don't ever say that, but that expectation is there. If that's not the case, you lose trust, you lose faith, and it's very hard physically and mentally.*

Linda shared how she uses the psychological contract with her classes at the University of Carleton. She explains to her students what she expects of them, and asks them to tell her what they expect of her as their professor. She explains how they will be graded and they discuss workload. She does this with every class so that students don't make assumptions, and she suggests that psychological contract exercises be done in the workplace to get these conversations on the table. From Duxbury:

> *What we know about the psychological contract is that any time there is a major shift around life cycle or promotion, you have to re-have that conversation.*
>
> *An employee can come into the company and be quite happy to travel all over the place and work 60 hours/week. And then they get married, and have a child and have different expectations. But the boss doesn't know the expectation has changed, so continues to give the employee travel. A psychological contract is a way to legitimize some of these dialogues and keep on top of them.*
>
> *This is a much healthier practice than performance review. The*

psychological contract is based on inputs and outputs. The employee gets from their organization rewards or outputs based on their input. But it should be an even ratio. I should get back proportional to what I put in.

When I put in more than I get out, things are out of whack. Work has evolved this way because of the baby boomers. Because we had more good people than good jobs. It's evolved to the point where expectations—especially of our managers and professionals—are totally unbalanced. We expect long hours, commitment and loyalty, and working on vacations and evenings, with pretty much nothing in return.

And that is the idea of a psychological contract. It must be a balanced set of ratios. When it is unbalanced, this causes stress, absenteeism, distrust, and all kinds of behaviours that are inappropriate because people feel they are not getting rewarded for their extra effort.

The Conversation is Never Done

Shain stresses that the conversation about psychological health in the workplace is never done:

I'm finding that when talking to leaders, the most important thing is to acquaint them with the need to have ongoing dialogue and conversation about where we're trying to go with psychological safety and health in the workplace. This is a conversation that must constantly be revisited. Sometimes you say something once, twice, maybe three times. And it's the fourth time where the light finally goes on. It's just the way people absorb knowledge.

To summarize, we're not in Kansas anymore. So, what is this new landscape we've landed in? It's hard to grasp it all at once. There's a lot of exploratory work that must be done. It's not exactly "over the rainbow" but it's certainly something quite different.

We all owe each other this duty of care to prevent harming one other mentally as well as physically. That narrative, as it begins to permeate the workplace, is a very powerful one. But getting the attention of CEOs is difficult. I find that what is useful is that once they set the ball rolling in relation to the Standard, there is an accountability mechanism. They're going to want to hear about how it's going. In the process of giving them feedback, there is an opportunity to reinforce the message. It's not a one-shot thing. It's a continuous conversation that involves senior leaders, and hopefully in the end gets them to galvanize into some more purposive action.

Shain is encouraged to have had the opportunity to see this process in action numerous times and says that it goes the right way more often than not.

Creating a psychologically safe and healthy workplace is not something we do well as a society. "We can do so much better," says Baynton. And Shain says we owe it to one another to prevent mental and physical harm in the workplace.

Keeping your workforce psychologically healthy and able to contribute their best makes good business sense. Inspiring mental wellness at work reduces the organization's risk of going in a vicious downward spiral and burning out our best people.

ACTIVITIES

Personal Practices:

1. Here are some questions to reflect on about your leadership practices and how they impact the psychological health in your workplace. Try picking one question each day and doing some focused writing on it in your journal.
   - Am I walking the talk?

- What are my hypocrisies as a leader when it comes to inspiring mental wellness at work?
- Do I role model good mental energy management?
- How is my own anxiety level? If high, what can I do to change this?
- How does the way I assign or schedule people to projects impact the balance in their lives?
- How does my language impact others' psychological health and safety?
- What deliberate move can I make today toward a more psychologically healthy culture?

2. The next time you are going through a major change with your immediate team, reflect on these questions used at Sinai Health System:
   - How am I reacting to the change?
   - What is my emotional state like?
   - Where am I in the change process?
   - How, then, am I going to be able to lead my team in a way that is healthy?

3. Personally fill out the Initial Scan (Stress Satisfaction Offset Score and Stress Satisfaction Index) found at www.guardingmindsatwork.ca to see what your score is. Use the tool with your teams or entire organization to assess these factors and get conversations going about what can be improved.

Team Practice:

Go through a psychological contract exercise with each of your team members. What do they believe or perceive about their obligations that are not in their legal employment contract? What do they expect from you as their employer or team leader in terms of workload, work-life balance and other assumptions? What can you expect from them?

Organizational Practice:

To "First, Do No Harm" to worker health, downloading and implementing the Standard (found at www.mentalhealthcommission. ca) is a starting point. Pay specific attention to the audits and assessments to develop a benchmark of where your organization's strengths and challenges are in terms of promoting psychological health.

But don't stop there. As Shain suggests, pull out the governance philosophy as a key factor to pay attention to. Develop and declare your vision and commitment as leaders to a "careful workplace."

Featured Influencer: Melissa Barton

Melissa Barton

Melissa is an energetic leader in the field of organizational health, safety and wellness with a wide variety of experience in healthy workplace strategy, policy and program development. She is passionate about working collaboratively to create best-practice healthy work environments and workplace cultures that inspire and transform the way organizations deliver their best possible value to their clients and communities.

Melissa holds a Bachelor of Science in Kinesiology from the University of Waterloo and a Masters of Business Administration from University of British Columbia. She has spent the majority of her career in the healthcare sector working at multiple academic hospitals, the Ontario Hospital Association (OHA) and the Quality Worklife-Quality Healthcare Collaborative (QWQHC), but has also worked in the private sector as the Global Wellness Manager with BlackBerry.

Melissa developed the OHA Healthy Hospital Initiative and led a consortium of 13 national healthcare organizations in the development of the QWQHC's Pan-Canadian Healthy Workplace Action Strategy for Success and Sustainability in Canada's Healthcare System.

She is currently the Director of Organizational Development and Healthy Workplace for Sinai Health System.

CHAPTER 9

VISION

"Every choice you make leads you away from your vision or moves you toward it."
—Patti Digh

Being the vision-keeper for positive change in your workplace is not always easy. As Dr. Robert Quinn has shared, in most organizations the prevalent mindset is more often about problem solving instead of possibility. But as a person leading change, if you can present an inspiring vision that engages people, the ripple effect can be infectious.

The reason we are talking about vision toward the end of this book and not at the beginning is that creating a compelling vision requires an understanding of why and how your culture needs to change. It also requires building the behaviours and practices to achieve it, which includes those we've discussed to this point: appreciative inquiry, transformational leadership, positive deviance, examining our hypocrisies as leaders, reflective action and so on.

The importance of positive vision came up repeatedly in the Thoughtexchange we held with the organizational health community. Many people concurred that what makes a workplace positive is a clear vision and purpose that people feel they can contribute to and are inspired to be a part of.

One respondent made this powerful comment: "You cannot create anything of value that will last for any meaningful length of time if it isn't desired or wanted by your people." It is essential to give everyone the opportunity to contribute to the vision.

From Lack of Vision to Seeing Possibilities

Recently I was working with the executive team of a large organization. They had organized a retreat off-site to do some visioning and team building. They recognized there was conflict, as well as other issues, keeping them from achieving their goals. The CEO was invested in increasing positivity in this team and had many concerns about the lack of communication and respect amongst team members.

We decided to have each team member complete the Aston Team Positivity Measure prior to the retreat.[79] As the scores came in one by one to me, I could see that there was a great deal of negativity (including cynicism and a focus on failures and difficulties) versus the encouragement, humour and celebration of achievement that characterizes positive teams. There were, however, some positive commonalities amongst the team, with the main one being the care and concern they had for their customers. This seemed like a great place to start our conversation.

I chose not to share the results of the Positivity Measure at the beginning of the retreat, but instead focused on the research around positive teams and the practices that increase positivity in organizations. I had also given them another pre-retreat assignment, which was to reflect on and come prepared to discuss the question "who are we when we're at our best?"

In the retreat, we heard everyone's reflections on this question and discussed which of these strengths were most important to build on as they moved forward with their new vision. We considered and practiced other ways of increasing team positivity, including gratitude, mindfulness, transformational questions and team debriefs. We asked the question, "What would make wellness possible in this workplace?"

When we finally turned to looking at the positive and negative scores, the team was having a good time. They were comfortable and positive, and had some tools in their pocket that they knew could help them move forward. The negativity of their scores did not phase them (I'm sure they were expecting them, and they were considering ways they could improve). The rest of the retreat was used to envision the future: where they wanted to be in six months, one year, and three years, and the practices they planned to put in place to start to create the culture that would help them get there.

Learning

In this situation, starting with evidence-based positive practices demonstrated to even the most disgruntled team member that there was hope, and that there was a positive way forward. Once people saw the value and impact of engaging in practices, it was easier to create a possibility-focused vision.

The story Dr. Quinn told us about the school district in Chapter Four shares a lot of similarities with this one. Once the participants in the school district session found their purpose, could see a new vision, and had a grasp of some practices that would be useful to move forward, new possibilities became apparent. As he says, there was not a more negative work situation than that one, and yet they found a hopeful way to move ahead.

In both cases, the transition from lack of vision to creating a new future was swift once a mechanism for change was understood. And in both cases, this included seeing the research and success from other organizations' experiences with positive people practices.

I asked many of the experts I interviewed for their advice on how to help organizations engage in setting a vision for a more positive workplace and how to live into that vision. Dr. Duxbury says that having the courage to set a vision and then stick with it and move it forward is something that defines a leader. "Visioning is iterative," she says. "It must speak to the heart. We need to pass it by a lot of people because where we start our vision may not be where our vision ends up. To capture people, they must see themselves in it."

She says that visioning is hard work and it takes time to do it well. People often go with a quick solution instead of visioning because it is easier and they feel they don't have the time. As Duxbury says, "Far too often we get people pumped up and then we shatter them." We ask for their input, but then we don't always follow through.

One suggestion she makes is to find out where your resistance is. She uses Lewin's Force Field Analysis to understand what the driving forces and restraining forces are within a group to any proposed change. This is a framework that has been widely used in business for over fifty years, and "looks at forces that are either driving movement toward a goal or blocking movement toward a goal."[80] She suggests that if the resistance to your new vision or change is massive, then don't go full steam ahead with it; instead, start with a small pilot first where you can demonstrate success and credibility and build trust from there.

> What do you want your culture to be?

Marie Mac Donald coaches leaders on setting their vision and says that often they will set vision for their business goals, but do not have one for the culture that is needed to achieve those goals. She does one-on-one coaching with these senior managers and holds them accountable to the culture they are trying to create. She then has them hold one-on-one meetings with each of their front-line supervisors to do the same thing. She says, "The vision of what you want your culture to be must be embedded in your business vision. It might be one line about being a healthy, positive, high-performing workplace, and then you break it down into goals, measures and accountabilities."

Dr. Gregor Breucker, keynote at the Conference in 2002, talked recently about the role vision played in a multi-year restructuring and culture change process with the BKK social health insurance system in Germany. BKK provides healthcare for about ten million German citizens through approximately 90 different organizations. Breucker manages the Division of Health Promotion there.

Part of what helped BKK through the restructuring and culture change process was the vision to develop an independent department of health promotion and prevention that focused specifically on workplace health. This division not only provides services to BKK's customers, but has also now begun providing workplace health services internally as well. This has been beneficial in helping to support positive culture change at BKK.

Breucker says the process they used has been mainly networking. They invited experts from within the BKK group of organizations to set up two networks: one for workplace health promotion, and the other for individual life-style related prevention outside of the workplace. They started with pilot projects in workplace health promotion. As Breucker says:

One of these was a series of partnerships between BKK organizations and regional employer organizations (Chambers of Commerce and local municipalities). The key joint activity is to organize local conferences for the needs of small workplaces. The results have shown that we can reach these small organizations that are a part of the BKK and support them with workplace health promotion in this way.

In our experience, the most important practices for shifting culture in our organization have been to introduce various networking opportunities which have a supplementary function in relation to the formal management mandate of a public sector social insurance institution under the supervision of the Ministry of Health.

It Starts with You

Imagining, brainstorming and creating vision is often the easy part. Achieving it takes constant communication and consistent practices. Quinn advises that for a vision to grow, you need to continually review, discuss and celebrate it.[81]

One way to get to the heart of your organization's vision and to keep the conversation going is to ask thought-provoking and transformational questions. When working with executives and teams to set their vision, Mary-Lou MacDonald uses inspirational questions that are grounded in the reality of her clients' industries.

I facilitate discussion with questions to queue their thoughts and help them express their vision for a more positive, healthy workplace. I use stories and examples of positive change from other organizations, which is also important to help them to see the possibilities. This is an approach that has been very successful, as many of the organizations I have used this process with have created sustainable positive change.

Here are four questions worth asking that can have a profound effect on creating a new vision for the culture of your organization.

1. What do we believe in?

Imagine the difference to your culture if everyone was tapped into the same purpose. Roy Spence, who keynoted for us at the Conference in 2011 and is the author of "It's Not What You Sell, It's What You Stand For," suggests asking the question "what do we believe in?"[82] He tells us that organizations driven by purpose and values regularly and reliably outperform their competition. Surveys consistently report that one of the most important criteria for attracting and retaining great people is a company purpose that makes them feel that what they do is important.[83]

If you haven't done this for a while (or ever) in your organization or team, get the conversation started by asking, "What do we believe in and what do we value?"

2. Who are we when we're at our best?

A great way to develop team vision is to ask, "Who are we when we're at our best?" What are the great moments we've had when we've performed the best we possibly could? The answer can be a very simple statement (e.g. "we create better workplaces" or "we provide the best healthcare") or a series of statements that together describe the vision of who we are when we are our best selves (e.g. we are mindful of how our actions impact our colleagues and our customers, we treat each other with kindness and respect, we give excellent service).

We used this question at our conference team retreats each year to continually renew, discuss and celebrate our vision and purpose going forward. It made us want to be our best more often, and it helped us to examine what was going well and how we could build on those strengths. Try it with your team. I guarantee it will change you.

3. What do we want our culture to be?

We discussed this question earlier in the book. It uses a visionary approach versus a problem-solving approach, and provides everyone the opportunity to have input into creating a great culture. It's time to ask this question.

As we've examined, this simple question was used at Baptist

Healthcare at a particularly low point in their history and resulted in moving their patient satisfaction from the 18th to the 99th percentile, cutting employee turnover in half and placing them in the top 25 in America's 100 Best Companies to Work For, every year now since 2002.

4. Are we solving problems or moving toward our vision?

Dr. Robert Quinn tells the story about one executive who wanted to keep focused on being purpose-driven. He hired a coach that he met with weekly, and that coach's sole job was to ask him this question each week: "Are you solving problems, or are you moving the institution?"

Why? Because, as Quinn explains, "In any administrative role, from a supervisor to the CEO of a company, there is an unconscious conspiracy wherein virtually everyone comes to you with problem solving. Most administrators spend all their time doing this. Many of them become addicted to it. It becomes their identity."

Remember the story Quinn told us earlier about the executive who wrote "what is the result you want to see?" on his white board? He was making the same shift from problem-solver to vision-keeper, as this CEO is trying to make. If you can find a way to pull out of problem-solving and keep focused on the purpose and vision of your work, as these executives have, you will be much more effective.

As you create a vision that will start shifting your culture in a positive direction, keep these four questions in mind. Use them at your next organizational or team retreat and notice what happens.

Ground it in Research

As the change agent in your organization, convincing other senior managers of the value of stepping away from conventional, problem-solving mindsets and toward living into a new vision may require sharing research and success stories from other organizations. As Dr. West says:

> *Senior management typically spend lots of time solving problems, reacting to challenges, and dealing with the difficulties. The question is how can we help them to really step back, sculpt a vision and be present with people to live that vision?*
>
> *I would say that the great success I've had over the last 15 years in influencing senior leaders in our healthcare system nationally is presenting them with clear evidence from our research that shows why it is important not only to articulate a vision, but to live it. The research shows that just articulating a vision and then going back to your daily business doesn't work.*

One of the most inspiring examples Dr. West shared with me was a series of courses his team ran with IBM called "Fit for the Future." They took leaders through a variety of visioning exercises, helping them to identify what their core motivations were in their work lives over the course of their careers, and then synthesized these into statements about what these leaders fundamentally stood for. From Dr. West:

> *This was profoundly moving for the executives. It was a privilege to observe. I think it's important that these leaders and managers regularly take time out and step back to do that kind of visioning process and to recognize that where they make the most difference is when they are focusing on core cultural values like those of compassionate leadership (attending, understanding, empathizing and supporting) rather than getting caught up in problem solving and dealing with difficulties. It is their function to enable the people they lead to deal with those other issues.*

Mary-Lou MacDonald also stressed the importance of providing statistics and background research to engage leaders in understanding the importance of investing in a healthy, positive culture. She has used the Stress and Satisfaction Offset Scale (SSOS) mentioned in the previous chapter to gather both individual and aggregate scores of how people are being impacted by stress.

> *In my last organization, 90% of the calls coming in to EAP were for stress. This is really important information to have. At the individual level, Health Risk Appraisals are also useful and can be motivational, especially when families get involved. As a leader, no matter what tool you use, you must be prepared to do something about it when the results come in.*
>
> *Communication about the results needs to be honest. In a company that I was a consultant to, the culture survey showed that the issues were with management style. The company tackled this and changes were made within leadership to address it. Re-testing later showed that this company reached the highest level of excellence due to attending to this one management issue.*
>
> *The key to developing and sustaining a new vision is leadership commitment; leaders integrating it into how they work personally and embedding new ways of doing things into the culture. There must be checks and balances in place that make it sustainable.*

Sustaining the Vision and Purpose

Spence tells us that a well-defined purpose drives all major decisions. It defines what we stand for, what we don't, and where we're headed. Knowing your purpose, vision and values allows you to run any big decision through the filter of "does this fit?"

Another way to sustain the vision is to encourage, promote and reward the behaviours and practices that support it. This starts with senior leaders demonstrating behaviours and practices that are consistent with the vision and the organization's values.

As Duxbury says, "We often talk about vision, but then we punish mistakes and differences." Instead, a great question to ask after a loss or setback is "what obstacles took us off-course, and how can we learn from them?" Part of becoming a learning culture is asking the tough questions and learning from our failures as well as our successes.

Some of the respondents to the Thoughtexchange shared ideas on sustaining the vision through things like forming an "Organizational Culture Team" or developing a charter that people were encouraged to sign which committed them to the agreed upon values in their daily behaviour at work.

Building a more resilient, effective workplace involves creating clear purpose and vision. Asking powerful questions is the starting point to creating that vision, and positive practices are the key to achieving it.

ACTIVITIES

Personal Practices:

1. Are your management skills more focused on problem-solving, or are you a more vision-focused leader? Pick a time of day when you can consistently take five minutes to turn to your leadership journal. Ask this question of yourself every day for a week: "Am I solving problems or moving the company forward?" Record your thoughts.

2. What is your personal vision for the culture in your organization or team in six months? One year? Three years? How can you use this question in a retreat or visioning session?

3. Take the four questions discussed in this chapter and reflect on them yourself first, then utilize them with your most immediate teams.
   - What do we believe in?
   - Who are we when we're at our best?
   - What do we want our culture to be?
   - Are we solving problems or moving toward our vision?

Team Practice:

Tailor the four questions used above to fit your team culture. Perhaps you send the questions out to people in advance of a meeting where you are going to discuss them, so that there is time to reflect on them. Perhaps you discuss one question each week for a month at your weekly meetings. Or, perhaps you plan an off-site retreat and use these questions as a basis for developing your team or organizational vision. Maybe you decide to coach each other on the fourth question, just as the CEO in this chapter had his coach ask him weekly.

Organizational Practice:

Develop a participatory network, such as an advisory group or networking group, to provide advice and guide your organization in developing and achieving your vision. What professionals and stakeholders would you invite to this group?

Featured Influencer: Dr. Gregor Breucker

Gregor Breucker

Dr. Gregor Breucker has been working for the Social Health Insurance System in Germany for the past 25 years. Currently he manages the division for health promotion at the Berlin BKK Federal Association of company health insurance funds.

In 1995, Gregor started to co-ordinate action at the European Union level on the framework of the first Public Health Programme by developing the European Network for Workplace Health Promotion. Part of this action was also to initiate corresponding network developments at national levels across Member States of the European Union.

His main focus is to use networking as a mechanism to disseminate good workplace health promotion practice. The new prevention law of the German government launched in 2016 set new incentives and requirements for more co-operation within companies and at the level of the various social insurance branches (pension, accident, health and labour market integration).

Gregor chairs a Social Health Insurance Consortium at the federal level which is responsible for the development of supportive infrastructures for smaller companies at the local and regional levels across Germany in the fields of workplace health promotion. He also co-ordinates internal networks within the BKK social health insurance system and company networks.

CHAPTER 10

Emergent Process

"Courage does not always roar. Sometimes courage is that quiet voice at the end of the day saying...I will try again tomorrow."
—Mary Anne Radmacher

I seem to need to learn the importance of trusting the emergent process over and over. It happened again while writing this book. There was the plan in my head of how the book would go, what the timeline would look like and when it would be done. And then there was the reality of how it developed.

When you embark on a book you have a vision of what it will look like, but as you begin researching and writing, the real book that needs to be written becomes apparent. I found this especially true as I conducted the speaker interviews. When I asked each speaker for a story, I believe that they each told the story they needed to tell, which is the case in this chapter. And as those stories shaped the book, the lessons and applications from each emerged.

Trusting the emergent process in this project is no different than trusting the process when you put positive practices in place in an organization. Some will work more easily than others, and some won't work at all, yet all will provide opportunities for learning. The culture will develop differently than you imagine, but it will emerge in a more positive way because of your effort and patience than it would if you

195

did nothing at all. It will also develop more positively using emergence than if you try to force the changes faster than they will naturally develop.

Conventional managers tend to try to take control of a situation to solve the problem, while transformational leaders solve issues through collective learning and trusting the emergent process. There is a time and place for both.

Trusting emergence takes us out of our comfort zone. Most people are more comfortable trying to predict the outcomes, even though we inherently know that in a people culture nothing is predictable. In his 2004 book "Building the Bridge as You Walk On It: A Guide for Leading Change," Dr. Robert Quinn describes how, while we may have a vision for what we'd like our culture to be, the path is not always apparent. We build as we go.[84]

Any change process in an organization relies on building bridges from our current state to where we want to be. The bridge is the emergent process, and trusting it requires using many of the transformational leadership practices we've already discussed throughout this book such as reflective action, positive deviance and mindful listening.

Building a Learning Culture

Marie Mac Donald is an executive and team coach. She coaches people on the concept of trusting the emergent process and, in the practice of this, on how to become a learning culture. It requires trial and error as we forge forward, learning from mistakes and developing the resilience and energy to try again. She stresses that mistakes are essential in a learning culture for building creativity and innovation. Where there is a fear of failure and punishment for "getting it wrong," there is less creativity to learn new ways of being.

Mac Donald worked with our Conference Team as an Executive Coach for many years. We built a learning culture by applying the key ideas that were being shared at the conference each year to our own team. She inspired us to "learn in the moment" as things were happening and continually strive to be a better team. The impact of this is evidenced in notes like the one below from one of our team members at the end her time working with us:

"Thank you for showing me how to do things 'better' not only in business, but in life. Thank you for giving me a chance. The past three years were a great balance of challenge, learning and fun, and I feel honoured to have been a part of it."
—Marta Devellano, Executive Assistant

Mac Donald also works with many other private and public organizations. In my interview with her she shared a story of building a culture of wellness and resilience in a public service agency that, in the end, helped them through an unimaginable incident. The work they were doing prior to this event is what she believes made it possible for them to carry on and continue to build a positive, learning culture afterward.

Marie's Story

I had been consulting with a public service agency for a couple of years. They were going through significant complex change, developing a new business model and a new executive team while also dealing with budget cuts, downsizing and layoffs. Everything was happening at the same time.

It was a stressful time for people, and I was initially called in to deliver change resilience workshops to staff. We didn't start with the mindset that we were going to change the culture. We were just amidst a very challenging situation and ended up trying some different techniques to find our way through it. This is how learning organizations operate.

For instance, one of the directors, who we'll call John, started coming to the sessions I was facilitating with staff. John had seen a very positive impact on a few people who attended these sessions and was eager to learn how he could support his staff and managers. Once he got the concept of how important the human side of change was, he readily agreed when I asked him if I could interview him in a "leadership chat" in these sessions so he could tell staff the background and rationale for the changes, how it would impact them and how much he needed their input to make it work.

I wanted John to show the team how much he cared about them, and that he needed their input on what his leadership team could do to lead through these changes more effectively. He came to all the staff sessions and did this.

I was also coaching him on the new role he was moving into. John and his new Executive Team (ET) asked me to work with their Divisional Management team which was a group of about sixty people. I led a couple of days on "Leading Change in a Complex Environment" with an emphasis on the human side and organizational health. This was a tough session for highly technical leaders because it was all new to them, but it was the beginning of a division cultural shift toward a learning culture.

Marie went on to tell me about the intensive work she did with this group. She helped them to follow through on their action plans and improve their communications while focusing on building individual and team resilience. She created a tool called the "Heart Battery" (Diagram 7) to help them visualize and be aware of where they each were in terms of stress and resilience, always aiming for the state of continual renewal found in the "comfortable" zone. This helped them to pay attention to workload, their input into changes that affected them, and other factors that affect stress levels.

DIAGRAM 7 The Heart Battery

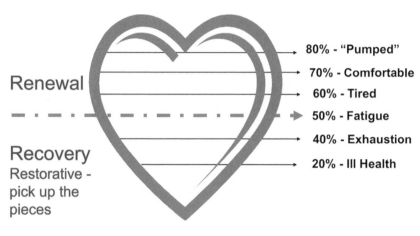

Heart Battery Level
Self awareness tool

Renewal

80% - "Pumped"
70% - Comfortable
60% - Tired
50% - Fatigue
40% - Exhaustion
20% - Ill Health

Recovery
Restorative -
pick up the
pieces

© Marie Mac Donald Consulting 2017

Marie could see early-on that this group was prepared to trust the emergent process and discover how to get through this change. They learned the importance of having supportive leadership from the top down. As she put it:

The ET owned the process. They were learners and did not need to be "knowers" (Knowers have a hard time creating a learning culture because they think they already know everything). They were confident, and so when I presented concepts of change leadership and Emotional Intelligence (EI) as a driver of becoming a learning culture, and psychologically healthy and safe workplaces, and how managing stress well would support health and resilience, they were wide open. I was attending The Better Workplace Conference regularly, and was sharing many ideas from there. I was their guide and learning along with them.

We began working with their whole leadership group, looking at what the business needed to transform and what the people needed at the same time. We talked about how to be effective as they moved through this change that was impacting every aspect of the work they did. They were very concerned about their people and about their business.

Marie shared a statement with me that the team developed as they were working through this change: **"The division places equal emphasis on its people and its business results. Our experience is that when you take care of your people, they will take care of the business even in turbulent times."**

This turned out to be a very prophetic statement when the day of the crisis came. Marie believes that the work they were doing to become a learning culture and to trust the emergent process is what helped them through the rest of this story.

I was on my way to one of their offices to lead some sessions and was going to meet with John that evening to debrief and finalize our plan for working with the teams the next day. I was at the airport heading out when I got the call.

There was a SWAT team at the office and it was locked down. There had been a shooting in the workplace. We knew that people were still alive as some were calling on their phones, but that is all we knew. They were trapped in a nightmare, and we were too—waiting to find out what had happened. The shooter's reasoning may never be known as he ended his own life as well, but the story here is not so much about the incident as about how the work we were doing was instrumental in helping get through this unimaginable tragedy where three people lost their lives.

John was one of them.

That night, instead of meeting with John to plan the meeting, I found myself huddled together with others on the team, heartbroken that this senseless tragedy had occurred. We ended up holding each other as we cried, not able to make sense of how this had happened.

As we tried to deal with our own shock and profound distress, the senior people in the organization and I began to plan for how we would support the team the next day. Every one of us was somehow feeling responsible. I felt then, and still do now, that it was like we were struck by lightning and fused together with the common goal of how we could carry on the work John started as our commitment to him. I am telling this story his memory.

The next day, we got all the staff together as planned. I called in a skilled social worker to come and support me and help facilitate a circle with all involved staff. We sat in a circle and she compassionately led us through an ongoing debrief. Everyone shared what had happened from their perspectives and how they were doing. It was striking that each person somehow felt responsible, feeling they should have been able to head this off. It turned out to be a common feeling for all involved. Counsellors were brought in and everyone was encouraged to take some private time with them.

The original plan was that Day One was to be a meeting with the regional team, and then Day Two with the leadership team from all over the province. We ended up using Day One for this very compassionate sharing, debriefing and supporting each other. Day Two was postponed for five weeks.

After extensive planning with the ET we brought all 60 of the leadership team back together five weeks later and we debriefed the whole issue with that group. We lived into an ironclad commitment to carry on John's work. We focused first on people and then on business. I brought in a consultant who was also a minister and a change expert. We talked about what had happened, and what the leadership thinking was behind it. We gave people an opportunity to talk about what the impact was on each of them and their teams.

There were tears and profound grief at the loss.

And that night, we sat in circle again to honour the people who lost their lives. We had a ceremony where people could speak if they wanted to, and we created a ritual to mark the ending where everyone wrote down what they needed to let go of to move ahead. Then we burned the paper. That was our closure. We said, "Tomorrow we focus on business and how we go forward."

Marie spoke of how everyone pulled together and supported each other in John's legacy. As they began to focus on how to move ahead with the business, they continued to touch on how people were doing throughout the day. Marie stresses that you can't separate the "people stuff" and the "business stuff" as so many organizations do; you must focus on both, together, in real time. As we carried on with our interview, I asked Marie if the culture continued to grow as it had started after this incident.

Before the incident, they were amidst a culture change and were extremely committed to seeing results, so afterwards they doubled their efforts to deal with this catastrophic event. We put a huge focus on resilience, because everyone was done in by this tragedy. I worked with the ET on their resilience intensely, including coaching and off-site meetings, and then we offered these team coaching sessions to all the staff in all the regions. Some of us worked with trauma therapists.

The ET committed to do whatever was necessary to make sure this never happened again, and they were doing it for John.

That's what put rocket boosters on the whole process. The ET was very transparent. Every three months I met with them to do "Walking the Talk" sessions. We focused on how they were doing, starting with a check in on their heart battery levels. They made commitments to each other and challenged each other to keep them.

It took well over a year before they could get above 50 (Fatigue).

They not only led this culture shift, they were open to designing it with me, learning from it, modeling it and acting with 100% integrity. We truly built the bridge while standing on it. Their decisions were made based on their business strategies as well as the culture they wanted to create. Nobody was hired into a leadership position, even at the lowest level, without fitting the culture.

In large group sessions we combined the business, the strategy, how things were going, and theory on how to become a learning culture. We were asking, "How do we get good at straight-talk with each other? How do we own our impact? What happens when you don't have control?" It was EI work we were doing. We were working on building change resilience using research that had been presented at the Conference and in the organizational development world.

We have discussed throughout this book the importance of self-transformation and shifting yourself first if you want to transform your team or organization. Marie stressed in this situation how important it was for anyone in a leadership position to learn to manage themselves first. She went on to work with the woman who replaced John to develop a Learning Performance Management Initiative (LPMI) for all the front-line managers and supervisors to help them deal with real business and people issues they were going through.

We developed and pioneered something we called Team EI Profiling using the Emotional Quotient (EQ) In-Action Profile and provided individual and team coaching with each of those managers and supervisors. We dealt with real issues in the moment. If there was a real issue going on in the province, we would practice what they were dealing with and they owned the process. We had a group of champions (front line supervisors and managers) within the organization that designed everything with us—they were our reference group throughout. When an issue was brewing, they named it and we brought it into the room.

They held their ground about hiring for culture. As each new leader moved on, the culture carried on. Their leadership really embodied the culture they wanted to create: a flexible, adaptable learning culture that did the best they could possibly do for the work they were doing.

The learning culture framework that I used with them all the way through was based on results, relationships and resilience. [See Diagram 8 below] Business results sit on your resilience and relationships. Individual resilience adds up to organizational resilience. This is hard, demanding work.

If you don't have resilience, you will not have the stamina to move through culture shift and transformational change. High performing, emotionally intelligent relationships are what drive performance. And if your resilience is low and your relationships suffer, guess what happens to your results?

DIAGRAM 8 The 3 R's of Performance

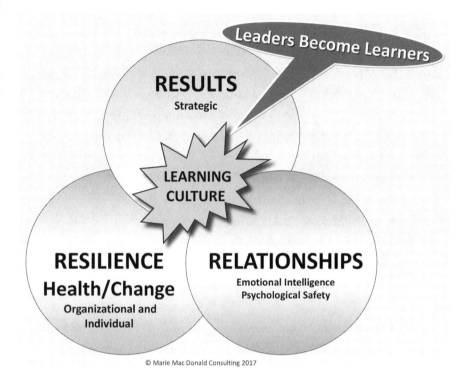

© Marie Mac Donald Consulting 2017

I asked Marie what advice she could provide to leaders who want to shift this way, and this was her response:

A focus on people in organizations has always been thought of as the "soft" or "easy" stuff, while the business is the "hard stuff." I suggest we let that go and focus on the people side of the business to power up performance on business results. I see the strategic focus as the "WHAT" of the business and the people focus as the "HOW." You can't do one without the other.

It's about having a learning mindset; giving yourself permission to learn along the way. As leaders, we've all been trained that "you have to have it right"; you must know exactly what you're going to do. But with the kind of complexity that organizations are dealing with now—and the complexity of doing your business while trying to create healthy, engaged, positive workplaces—you must learn your way through that with all levels of your organization.

The leadership team must do their own deep examination of whether they are prepared to be models. They need to be the full-on executive sponsors of change. If they don't walk, talk and act with integrity, it's very difficult to get a full-scale shift. This is the EI work. Often what you will find is that people who really embrace the learning culture get better at being leaders and bring in better business results and high levels of engagement.

A key element is taking strategic reflection time to regularly go off-line and reflect on what's going on right now. I suggest asking:

- *What just happened here?*
- *What does it mean to us?*
- *What are we going to do about it?*

Everyone needs to put everything in and shift away from the "command-control, we've-got-to-get-it-right every time, blaming" mindset toward a more curious, engaged, empowered learning organization.

When a team of strong leaders decided to honour a fallen colleague, the sky was the limit. They walked and talked it and grew themselves and their organization. I had the great honour of walking beside them for more than nine years while they led courageously.

In the tough times, I kept quoting:

"It is supposed to be hard. If it wasn't hard everyone would do it…it's the hard that makes it great." *—Tom Hanks from the movie A League of Their Own*

and [the quote at the beginning of this chapter]:

"Courage does not always roar. Sometimes courage is that quiet

voice at the end of the day saying...I will try again tomorrow."
Mary Anne Radmacher

Marie's story exemplifies how developing a learning culture and trusting the emergent process can become the road that helps a team to move forward. She outlined six fundamental principles that helped this department develop a learning culture and continue onward after this incident. They are:

- The people side and the business side go hand in hand.
- Leadership EI is an essential driver of a learning culture.
- Mistakes are essential. We learn from them, and this is how we increase creativity and innovation.
- Resilience is central to change and transformation.
- It is critical for the senior people to walk the talk and to lead the change, as well as defend their people.
- Helping people find closure after a significant event is vitally important.

> How can you create a culture where employees can contribute their best?

Finding Language That Helps Us Grow

In a learning culture, leaders ask questions after a setback or disappointment; this practice can be transformational in helping people move forward positively. In Brené Brown's company, Daring Greatly, they have developed a series of questions to ask after every failure or setback. As Brown explains in her book "Rising Strong: The Reckoning. The Rumble. The Resolution," they use questions to learn from their mistakes, such as "what emotions are people experiencing?" and "what do we need to get curious about?"[85] This is part of what they call their "rumble," and it has become a part of their language. If a team member has a concern about something, they can simply suggest there be a "rumble" on that item at the next meeting.

What if all companies created language like this, and it was OK for any employee to question a process or a new direction by suggesting a rumble? What a difference that would make.

At one of our Conference Team retreats, we looked at the language we were using, both in terms of how language was limiting us and how we could use new language. We brainstormed all the limiting words and phrases we used. People wrote down expressions like "because we've always done it that way," and "the problem with that is…" and so on. We shared these phrases out loud, laughed about them, put them all in a jar and literally "put a lid on them," vowing to catch ourselves anytime we used this limiting language.

This was a part of how we were endeavouring to create a healthy learning culture. The biggest challenge for our Conference Team was that we were not a team of employees from the same company with one culture, but that we were a team made up of representatives from many small businesses, each with their own culture. These cultures could easily infiltrate into our team culture, and sometimes did.

There is a story about this that I want to end with. The story is about a woman who provided administrative support, logistical support and registration services to the Conference Team. Alison represented PRIME, the event planning company that we contracted to manage the logistics of the conference. She was a great team player and became very passionate about what we were trying to achieve through this forum.

Event planning companies are excellent at getting things done and doing high quality work, and we worked with PRIME for 14 years because of their ability to provide such great service. In the early years though, we found that there was a personal price attached to that great service for the event planning staff. Their conscientiousness meant they often worked all hours to get things done, and then at conference time they could be exhausted and maybe even sick. So, we were working on that—changing practices and trusting the emergent process.

Jonathan, the President of PRIME, also sat on our team and was recognizing that at this wellness-focused conference, it was vitally important for his team to show up rested and well. At this time, PRIME was starting to schedule differently for all their conferences, making sure that the staff showed up healthy and had appropriate breaks throughout the events. They were enjoying the way we ran our meetings, and started to apply some of our positive meeting principles to their other client events as well.

It was during this time, however, that something happened with Alison. She had been working on several different events, ours included, and was feeling overwhelmed. I had completely forgotten about the situation, but last January on Bell's Let's Talk Day I got a message from her. She had moved away to another province and we hadn't been in touch for about eight years. She sent the following message that she gave me permission to share with you here:

Hi Deb,

With today being Bell's Let's Talk Day, I couldn't help but reflect on the struggles I've faced and look back at the people who supported me and helped me find the tools and the help I needed to get out of that dark hole. So, I want to say THANK YOU for being one of those people.

I'll never forget telling Jonathan and you that I didn't think it was a good idea for me to work onsite at the Conference that year in Vancouver. I felt like I was letting you down, but knew it would be worse if I broke down and "lost it" while working at the registration desk of a Health, Work and Wellness Conference (not good PR). And it meant so much to me when you insisted I come to the conference regardless, so I could listen to some of the presentations & speakers and be surrounded by the positive messaging. I still have my autographed copy of Rosamund Zander's book, "The Art of Possibility," that you gave me.

I've had my ups & downs since then, but through reading, counselling, meditation, various workshops and initiatives like Bell's Let's Talk, I've never been in a better place mentally & emotionally. But it all started with my very first advocate for wellness—so I send you a heart-felt Thank You!!

Best,
Alison

When I recalled the conversation, I remembered how much the Conference meant to Alison. Knowing this, it felt like inviting her to attend as a delegate was the right thing to do. Even though she was unable to work there, she had helped create the event and been a big part of it. Thankfully Jonathan supported the decision too. Not only did he support her to attend so that she could be surrounded by the like-minded, uplifting community at this event and listen to the positive messages from the speakers, but he also approved her attendance at one of our next conferences. She wasn't working as a part of our team anymore, but instead she was representing PRIME and participating as a delegate.

Part of developing our learning culture and trusting the emergent process was to tackle these situations head on and to make the best decisions we could as we moved forward. We often never know how our actions, positive or negative, impact others.

Rosamund Zander, the author of the book Alison mentions, was our opening keynote at the conference that year. One question she asked in that keynote that really stood out for me was "who am I being that my employees' eyes are not shining?"[86] Or, one could also rephrase this in the positive: "who can I be that my employees' eyes ARE shining?" or "how can I create a culture where we learn from mistakes, so that employees can exceed expectations?"

As you answer these questions and develop personal, team and organizational practices to create that culture, you will likely be moving into unchartered territory. Trust the emergent process as you do this and just notice what happens. If needed, you can always change course.

ACTIVITIES

Personal Practices:

1. Get your journal or blank note pad for some focused writing and set a timer for five to ten minutes. Consider the question "who can I be that my employees' eyes shine?" and begin to write what comes to mind.

2. Take another five to ten minutes of focused writing to go back to what you want your culture to be, contemplating this question: "How can I create a culture where we learn from mistakes so that employees can exceed expectations?"

3. When you review your through-line this week, ask yourself if the answers to your questions above change your first three turns for the week. Add any relevant thoughts that come up from this process to the "someday list" in your personal leadership plan.

Team Practice:

Identify an issue your team is dealing with right now. Develop a transformational question to:
  1. help people think differently or more positively about the situation,

2. inspire them to take on this new challenge, and/or
3. help them to get engaged in the new vision.

Start by focusing on what is going right. Facilitate the discussion that answers the question that you ask, and trust the emergent process as you go.

Organizational Practice:

Now take the above team practice to the organizational level. Teach the leaders in your organization how to lead emergent processes. The practice below was adapted from Robert Quinn's "The Positive Organization."[87]

Identify a challenge your organization is grappling with now. Facilitate an emergent discussion with the senior leaders in your organization to address this challenge. Use these questions as guidelines:

- How can I develop a transformational question to focus our leaders on our vision versus focusing on the problem?
- What is the result we want to create?
- What are the strengths of our organization that will help us deal with this challenge?
- How can I keep people focused on the possibilities, and continually bring the conversation from the negative back to the positive?
- How can I empower the leaders to own the process?

Quinn suggests that if you are not comfortable teaching or leading this process in your workplace, an alternative is to bring in a process facilitator to help. Marie Mac Donald acted as a process facilitator to the organization in this chapter's story.

Find a way to help every leader in your organization learn to lead the emergent process well in order to develop a learning culture.

Featured Influencer: Marie Mac Donald

Marie Mac Donald
BSc., MSW

Marie Mac Donald is a dynamic executive coach, consultant, facilitator, educator and keynote speaker working across Canada to support the development of healthy, high performing workplaces. She is an effective strategist who partners with her clients to clarify their visions and key priorities—and then achieve them. Marie's expertise in individual and team Emotional Intelligence profiling, complex change, leadership resilience and developing learning cultures provides a solid platform from which she can provide support and guidance to her clients.

Marie uses her extensive professional and personal experience to both inspire and challenge with a great sense of humour, warmth and empathy. She has a gift and a passion that makes it fun and keeps it real with her motivating and practical approach.

Certified by the Canadian Mental Health Association as a Psychological Health and Safety Adviser in 2015, Marie was among a group of consultants chosen from across Canada to pilot the national certification program.

As a speaker, Marie brings a powerful blend of hard and soft skills from her 28 years' experience working with individuals and organizations. She customizes her approach with leading edge techniques grounded in resilience. Marie believes that business results are grounded on resilience and high trust relationships.

Find out more about Marie's work at www.mariemacdonald.com.

CHAPTER 11

Best Advice & Tools

"When everything seems to be lacking in integrity, you find it in yourself. You change the world right where you are standing."
—Quote from the TV show Madam Secretary, 2015.

What would happen if you put each of the practices introduced in this book in place in your workplace, in no particular order, tailoring each to fit, using your through-line and asking, "What are my next three turns?" As we've heard from the Featured Influencers throughout this book, it is so much easier to manage a company this way.

As you implement the practices discussed here, continually check in with yourself and your team. Go back to the question that forms the through-line of this book: "What will we do differently to create a better place to work?" Then ask yourself, what will our story be in one year? Two years? Five years?

What Can We Do Differently to Create a Better Place to Work?

The experts that I interviewed were all asked for their best recommendation in answer to this question. Following is a synopsis of what they had to say.

1. Become a transformational leader

From Robert Quinn: "There are two worldviews. One is the conventional worldview that most people use. The other is the positive worldview that brings possibility to constraint, and is inclusive. It includes problem solving, but brings purpose finding to it. People often get there through traumatic life experiences. It's time to go all the way into the high schools and to help people embrace higher purpose in their lives, and their careers, and to bring a positive framework and a bilingual leadership mindset to people long before a mid-life crisis hits. We have to accelerate the learning process about something that almost no one understands, and that's a very big challenge."

From Mary Ann Baynton: "The number one thing is that we need to focus on developing solutions instead of identifying problems. Whenever we get into 'management approach' or an organizational structure that focuses on fear or pointing out people's faults, we're going to have challenges in the system. Where we have a system that focuses on strengths and solutions for employees to be successful—this shift in approach makes a difference. If we ask, 'Am I really trying to support this employee to be successful or am I trying to find fault?' we can shift a culture."

2. Shift to a foundation for psychological health

From Martin Shain: "CEO's, Boards and Owner-Managers need to recognize that we've entered a new era in labour relations in which there is an assumed duty to protect the mental health of workers. This is going to take its place alongside the general duty of care that already exists in Occupational Health & Safety (OH&S).

"The first thing we need to do differently is to see differently. Doing the right thing needs to flow from seeing things in an appropriate way.

In my work, I ask people to focus on properly formulating the problem, because when you do that it will usually suggest its own solution.

"When I'm working with organizations that are implementing the Standard, I constantly circle back to the original understanding (that there is an assumed duty to protect the mental health of workers), because it's so easy for a working group to devolve into the checklist way of doing things.

"We need to continually revisit the spirit of why we are trying to modify the way we behave toward each other in the workplace. That is the upstream driver of the Standard. So, the CEO and the Board need to send a clear message—not only through word, but also through behaviour that they are taking it seriously.

"This is a new chapter in the development of the employment relationship that began 150 years ago with the OH&S Acts, and it's finally taking the protection of mental health into this framework."

3. Reward what we value

From Linda Duxbury: "The misalignment comes when we say we value our people, work-life balance and employee health, but we reward and recognize long hours, imbalance and never saying no. If we truly want to move forward with these issues, we must align what we say we value, with what we recognize, promote and reward."

4. Determine our desired state

From Mary-Lou MacDonald: "I used to focus on strategy and 'what is the current state,' but I now focus on helping the organization determine 'what is the desired state?' and 'what is the motivation for change?' The pain points creating the desire to change culture could be morale, or a new CEO. It will be different for every organization, but it's important to determine what it is for yours.

"I facilitate exercises with organizations to help them work through what their desired state is, what their motivation to change is, and help them define how they want to feel. Just as it is important for individuals to understand how we want to feel in our lives when we embark on change, organizations need to go through the same process. They need to then move to 'what actions do we need to take to get that feeling?' Determining the 'desired state' for organizations also includes the outcomes we want to have, such as organizational viability or cost-savings."

5. Create a learning culture

From Marie Mac Donald: "We need to give ourselves permission to learn our way into our desired culture. How will we do this together? What is the leading-edge research telling us? We don't need to start at zero, we can learn from the innovators. Work with the front-runners. And then, as Kotter suggests, how do you connect the army of volunteers within your organization that want to create a learning culture in a safe, high-trust way?[88] I connect people within the organizations I work with; connecting this person to that person because they are on the same track. We grow each other in real-time learning."

6. Be a compassionate leader

From Michael West: "Develop compassionate leadership. There are four behaviours involved in that: attending, understanding, empathizing and supporting. This is what the role of leadership is critically about. We need to start to develop these models of leadership."

7. Initiate conversations

From Graham Lowe: "People who are in positions that influence the overall HR strategy need to have the conversation about creating a healthy culture. They need to start these discussions with their colleagues and find like-minded people in the organization who can work together collaboratively to identify the best opportunities to make progress. It's simple. There's nothing complicated about it. It's just being able to initiate conversation and frame it in a way that it is relevant to where the organization is at and where it wants to go."

8. Value others

From Gregor Breucker: "Create and develop opportunities in all relevant domains of working and non-working life to ensure that human beings can build up an integrated and self-valuing self-concept, which allows them to value other human beings and to build adult relationships in their families and all other relevant communities.

"A positive culture in my understanding requires certain qualities of personal development in leaders and teams, a high capacity for empathy, self-reflection, and an adult approach to aggression and conflict based on a high capacity to self-value."

9. Create more space for reflection

From Melissa Barton: "We need to consciously create more space for reflection. Reflective capacity increases tolerance for the ambiguity and uncertainty that happens in workplaces. Higher reflective capacity is also associated with a reduction in reactivity. Reactivity is responding reflexively in a manner that reduces one's capacity to look at potentially stressful events in fuller context. By increasing reflective capacity, we can generate a broader and more effective range of potential interpersonal responses—building better interpersonal relationships and better workplaces."

What is Your Most Highly Recommended Tool for Shifting Culture?

Each expert was also asked to share his or her most highly recommended tool for shifting culture. The answers were somewhat surprising. I guess I was stuck in conventional thought and expecting a list of assessments, audits, tests, and other such tools. But given the experience of those I interviewed in shifting culture, the tools they most recommended were more often "ways of being," or practices, which is what this whole book has been about. So, we've come full circle.

Any resources mentioned below can be found in the Resources Section.

Integrity

For example, when I asked Robert Quinn this question I was expecting he would recommend the tool he developed called "The Positive Organization Generator" (POG) which we introduced in Chapter Four. It is a fantastic tool, and I even went so far in the interview as to say, "I assume you will recommend this tool." He responded with, "No, definitely not! The POG is a great tool, but…" and he went on to say this: **"The first and foremost tool for bringing cultural change, is me increasing my own integrity and then getting other people from the organization to increase their integrity."**

Of course, when he said this I realized that this is exactly the point. Every positive change I've ever experienced in a workplace has come about through someone finding their integrity and working to help others find theirs. When we move together with integrity toward our vision of a better culture, there will be no stopping us.

Create Learning Cultures

Marie Mac Donald says that becoming a positive, healthy workplace requires leaders to grow their capacity to create learning cultures. Her most highly recommended tool is having a mindset that says "we have to learn our way through complexity. There is no other way." To do this, leaders must learn about their own Emotional Quotient (EQ). She recommends the EQ In-Action Profile tool for this purpose.

Communicate Continuously

"People need to talk all the time. Culture change is the most difficult type of change there is, and often you don't get the change because people don't see the need or the sense of urgency," says Linda Duxbury. She uses the Lewin's Forcefield Analysis introduced in Chapter Nine to establish the case for change.[80]

> We get stalled when trying to change because the forces pushing for change are sometimes outweighed by the forces resisting it. I ask a series of questions from those going through the change to try to understand the forces, such as:
> - Why do you think the organization is doing this?
> - What is driving the organization to change?
> - What is stopping the organization from changing?

Lewin's Force Field Analysis provides a clear view of the barriers and the drivers of change at different levels within the organization.

Effectively Deal With Conflict

Mary Ann Baynton recommends an interviewing technique that we introduced in Chapter Seven for dealing with conflict. The questions she uses are:

1. What is already good about this place that you wouldn't want to lose if there were to be some changes?
2. What would need to change for you to be excited about coming to work, supported to do a good job, and able to leave with energy at the end of the day?
3. What would you be willing to do differently, to reach your goal in the previous question?
4. If for some reason, you were having a bad day and not following the shared expectations that will be developed from these interviews, how would you want others to approach you about it or what do you believe would be a reasonable consequence?

Using the answers to these questions, she suggests developing an agreement or charter that everyone can sign off on and hold each other accountable to.

Develop a Participatory Network Methodology

Gregor Breucker says that there are various tools and concepts that they have used to shift culture. He would pull these together in the description "participatory network methodology."

This simply means to invite the relevant stakeholders—such as company-based stakeholders as well as representatives of employer organizations, trade unions, business sector organizations and governmental organizations—to join a networking process which allows for interested stakeholders to contribute their own views and experiences and take over shared responsibility for the network.

Cultivate Awareness, Understanding and Carefulness

Martin Shain recommends a set of evidence-based cultural tools he conceived and originated called the Neighbour at Work Imperatives. These tools are based on three principles: awareness, understanding and carefulness. Each one involves practices, and they are building blocks of a psychologically safe and healthy culture. Martin says:

> *Awareness means being aware of how I affect you and you affect me, and trying to increase in that capacity. Understanding is the recognition and reasonable accommodation of one another's legitimate needs, rights and interests. Based on these two factors we can become more "careful" with one another, in the sense of avoiding reasonably foreseeable harm to one another.*

In addition, Martin sees the new National Standard of Canada for Psychological Health and Safety in the Workplace as expressing the vision and aspirations of the "careful workplace," which he defines as one that conserves individual, social and economic capital by allowing no foreseeable negative mental health to workers.[76] As Martin says, "The Standard is a vehicle for creating and delivering the careful workplace."

Assess Stress and Satisfaction In Your Workplace

Melissa Barton recommends the Standard as well. Within the Standard is a tool that she has found very useful in starting conversations about the balance between stress and satisfaction at work called the Stress and Satisfaction Offset Score, developed by Martin Shain

She also recommends poetry as a very powerful tool, such as the Poetry in Residence program used at Sinai Health System.

Develop Personal Awareness

Mary-Lou MacDonald says that shifting culture comes down to personal awareness:

> *I often see individuals in the workplace who don't understand their own triggers, motivations, goals and desires. If we want people to be high performing both mentally and physically, they need to have a basic awareness of what makes them tick psychologically and physically. They need personal awareness of the implications of their behavior.*

One tool she recommends that synthesizes the self-awareness of everyone in the organization and gives you an aggregate score is called the Culture Index.

Define Behaviours That Enliven Your Values

Graham Lowe says that his approach has always been to encourage organizations and change agents to come up with their own tools. He says, "Breathing life into the values and really understanding the kinds of behaviours that are going to most exemplify those values is important. Increasingly, organizations are putting indicators of values into their surveys."

Nurture Compassion and Positivity

When asked for his most highly recommended tool, Dr. Michael West recommended creating positive environments and increasing compassion at work:

There are two tools I would recommend: compassion is one, and positivity is the other. We need to work to create positive environments and help people feel valued, respected, supported, and to feel optimism, gratitude, humour and cohesion. Our emotions are so important to us as a species. If we ignore the importance of emotion in organizations, which we very often do, people are stuck in their thoughts and intellect, and we make a big mistake. We must create positive environments. We must create environments of respect, inclusion, tolerance and valuing people. Compassion is a route to doing that effectively.

There were more than 50 leadership practices introduced in this book. They are a mixture of individual, team and organizational practices that can be tailored to shift culture in your workplace to one where people can flourish. These practices are listed again in the Resources section for your reference.

After reading the stories and recommendations in this book, consider these questions that were posed throughout the chapters, as you move forward:

What will we do differently to create a better place to work?

How will your workplace be different tomorrow if there is a positive shift today?

What leadership practices will you adopt to create a positive people culture?

How can you be positively deviant today?

What can your organization do to enhance team performance?

What practices can you implement that will be different from 'the way we've always done things' and lead to a better way to do business in the future?

What change can you make personally to embody the culture that you want to see?

What leadership practices can you start today to create positive upward spirals in your team or organization?

What can you do today to start a shift toward maximizing mental energy for all in your workplace?

What do you want your culture to be?

How can you create a culture where employees can contribute their best?

In January 2014, as I was making note of my goals for the year in my journal (and thinking about starting to write this book) I found myself writing this question:

What will you do differently to achieve these goals?

If you have the goal of a better team, a better culture, a better organization, or better leadership skills, what will you personally do differently to contribute to that goal?

I have also lived the story that I wanted to tell here. I have experienced the need from within organizations for a better way to do business, engaged in the practices taught here and noticed positive change, practiced positive deviance to transform cultures, and used the positive organization principles in my work.

I have learned over and over the need to shift myself first if I want others to follow. I've learned from burnout, and from coming back strong from it. I've seen how the practices of gratitude and mindfulness ignite positivity, and what that does to my creativity, energy, and zest for life.

I am doing my part to make psychological health a part of the work conversation. It has been thrilling to watch teams transform through the practices described here and to watch learning cultures grow when people are asked the right question at the right time.

There is a wonderful quote by a character in George Bernard Shaw's play "Back to Methuselah" that goes: "You see things and say, 'Why?' But I dream things that never were and say, 'Why not?'"

To me, that is the essence of possibility: having a dream, a vision of what might be, and saying "Why not?"

Why not create a better place to work? Why not let the driver of that change be you?

Why not?

It is so easy to succumb to the negative that is so powerfully and potently around us in this world. But find the positive stories. They are there. Some of them are here within these pages.

Immerse yourself in the positive practices and live the story you want to create.

Resources

Chapter 1

Practices introduced:
- Using focused writing to develop new, creative ideas
- Using the through-line approach as your personal leadership plan
- Examining the costs of doing nothing in your organization

Chapter 2

Practices introduced:
- Creating a bold vision
- Practicing positive deviance (deviating from the norm in a positive way)
- Using transformational questions as a form of appreciative inquiry:
  - What do we want our culture to be?
  - Why do we exist? (mission)
  - What are we striving to become? (vision)
  - What guides our everyday behavior? (values)
  - What do my employees think that I think is important?
  - How do they know? (Am I talking about what is important to me? Am I leading by example?)
  - Who am I when I am at my best?
  - Who are we as a team when we are at our best?
  - How will I be a contribution today?
  - In what ways do I want to become a more transformational leader?
  - What is the transformational question I need right now?

- Engaging employees in change processes.
- Forming a team of like-minded individuals who share your vision.

Chapter 3

Practices introduced:
- Contemplating ways of becoming a more transformational leader. (How do you see yourself leading differently a year from now? What steps are you willing to take to shift toward a more transformational leadership style?)
- Examining your hypocrisies as a leader
- Incorporating reflective action in how you lead and encouraging it in meetings
- Reviewing the organizational health efforts in your organization to examine:
  - o Is there a focus on culture shift or a program focus?
  - o Are efforts aimed downstream or upstream?
  - o Do we have more conventional management practices or transformational leadership practices?
  - o In what ways can these efforts be shifted?

Chapter 4

Practices introduced:
- Gap analysis between your future team or organization and where you are now.
- Incorporating the principles of positive organizing:
  - o Inviting people to find their purpose.
  - o Engaging them in authentic conversation.
  - o Empowering them to see possibility.
  - o Focusing on the common good.

o Trusting the emergent process.

Tools introduced:
- The Positive Organization Generator. The "quick assessments" from this tool are included at the end of Chapter Four, but for the rest of the tool see Quinn's "The Positive Organization" or http://www.liftexchange.com/generator.

Chapter 5

Practices introduced:
- Developing resilient cycles to replace your vicious cycles.
- Asking yourself what patterns and practices you need to let go of, continue and/or start.
- Incorporating appropriate breaks in your day to maintain energy.
- Developing email intelligence.
- Disconnecting from work frequently.
- Developing better sleep habits.
- Rewarding the behaviours that you want in your culture.

Chapter 6

Practices introduced:
- Assessing your personal positivity ratio and developing practices to improve it. Go to the tools section at www.positivityresonance. com to assess and track your positivity ratio as you introduce new positive practices.
- Increasing positive emotion personally, in your teams and throughout your organization through gratitude practices.
- Developing a meditation practice. (For example, try Jon Kabat-Zinn's body scan meditation. See www.mindfulnesscds.com.)
- Learning how to mindfully listen.

- Teaching mindfulness in your organization.

Chapter 7

Practices introduced:
- Assessing whether you have real teams or pseudo teams in your workplace.
- Developing an agreed upon set of team practices.
- Improving team reflexivity, particularly social reflexivity in your teams.
- Measuring the positivity in your team and developing practices to improve it. (See the Aston Team Positivity Measure below.)
- Engaging in team debriefs.
- Empowering people to find better ways of working.
- Learning emotional intelligence skills.
- Hiring for culture-fit.
- Using a positive, question-based practice to work through team conflict, such as the questions Mary Ann Baynton uses below.

    1. What is already good about this place that you wouldn't want to lose if there were to be some changes?

    2. What would need to change for you to be excited about coming to work, supported to do a good job, and able to leave with energy at the end of the day?

    3. What would you be willing to do differently to reach your goal in the question above?

    4. If for some reason, you were having a bad day and not following the shared expectations that will be developed from these interviews, how would you want others to approach you about it or what do you believe would be a reasonable consequence?

Tools introduced:

Aston Team Positivity Measure
©Aston Organisation Development Ltd 2013

There is considerable evidence that the ratio of positivity to negativity experienced by team members in their interactions at work has a significant impact on the well-being of the individuals and the team's ability to succeed in achieving required work outcomes. The **Aston** team positivity ratio provides an assessment of the team's current climate based on team member feedback about behaviour and mood in the team over the previous month.

Instructions

Have each of your team members complete the following questionnaire using the 1 to 5 scale below.

1.Strongly 2. Disagree 3. Neither agree 4. Agree 5. Strongly agree
  disagree   nor disagree

Tick the box below which best represents your opinion about team members in your team

Members of my team...	Strongly disagree	Disagree	Niether agree nor disagree	Agree	Strongly agree
	1	2	3	4	5
1...willingly provide support for each other					
2...complain about the contribution of other team members					
3...celebrate the team's achievements					
4...are cynical about the team's work					
5...celebrate each other's achievements					
6...express doubtls about the team's ability to succeed					

7...are enthusiastic about the team's vision					
8...dwell on failures and difficulties					
9...encourage each other to succeed					
10...talk about the obstacles they see at work					
11...joke and laugh together					
12...talk about their wish to leave the team					

Sum the totals across all team members for answers to the **positive** items 1,3,5,7,9,11 and divide by six (the number of items)

Sum the totals across all team members for answers to the **negative** items 2,4,6,8,10,12 and divide by six (the number of items)

Divide these two figures by the number of people who completed the questionnaire and you can then use this information to assess the climate for positivity in your team. You will have two figures between 1 and 5. Enter the results below.

Team Name:
Number of team member responses:
Number of team members invited to respond:
Results

Your team average positivity score:

Your team average negativity score:

Average scores for each of the two dimensions will be between 1 and 5 The overall ratio of reported positive to negative features in your team indicates the likely health and effectiveness of your team now and in the future.

An average positivity score of 4 and above suggests your team is generally highly positive and likely to be optimistic, effective, innovative and cohesive.

An average positivity score of 3 or below suggests low levels of optimism, cohesion and efficacy and this will affect team performance and team member health and well-being negatively.

An average negativity score of 3 or above suggests a high degree of cynicism and pessimism and an expectation of team failure. This will have a negative impact on team member health and well-being as well as on team performance.

How to increase your Team Positivity:

- Celebrate individual and team achievement and note what it was about the team's behaviour that enabled success.
- Talk more about what is going well.
- Use differences in opinion as opportunities to improve quality and build team resilience. Avoiding issues always leads to impaired team functioning in the longer term.
- Encourage the use of positive language – highly performing teams have six times more positive interactions and use more positive language than negative. Poorly performing teams use more critical and negative language than positive; team member interactions are also more likely to be negative.
- Take time out to reflect on performance and to adapt processes and behaviours to achieve required outcomes.
- Show interest in, and support for, team colleagues as individuals.

> • Ensure that the team's structure and processes are appropriate and effective – you may wish to carry out an assessment using an evidence-based diagnostic tool such as the Aston Real Team Profile+ or the Aston Team Performance Inventory.

This tool was provided with permission from Aston OD. For more information about other team diagnostic and development tools visit: www.astonod.com.

Chapter 8

Practices introduced:
- Setting a foundation for psychological wellness by:
    - o Making psychological health a continual part of your workplace conversations.
    - o Declaring your vision and commitment to transform culture.
    - o Maximizing mental energy for all employees.
    - o Developing psychological contracts with your employees.
- Reflecting on and improving your leadership practices as they relate to psychological health. (e.g. Am I walking the talk? Do I role model good mental energy management? How does my language impact others' psychological health and safety?)
- As you move through change, reflecting on:
    - o How am I reacting to the change?
    - o What is my emotional state like?
    - o Where am I in the change process?
    - o How, then, am I going to be able to lead my team in a way that is healthy?

Tools introduced:
- The Guarding Minds@Work (GM@W) Initial Scan is a free assessment that can be found on the GM@W website (www.

guardingmindsatwork.ca). It generates two scores, the SSOS (Stress and Satisfaction Offset Score) and the SSIX (Stress and Satisfaction Index), and information on how to interpret results is provided.

- National Standard of Canada for Psychological Health and Safety in the Workplace (download from: www. mentalhealthcommission.ca)

Chapter 9

Practices introduced:
- Developing a shared possibility vision with your people, asking questions such as these:
    - o What do we believe in?
    - o Who are we when we're at our best?
    - o What do we want our culture to be?
    - o Are we solving problems or moving toward our vision?
- Developing leadership skills that are more focused on vision than problem-solving.
- Developing a participatory network, such as an advisory group or networking group, to provide advice and guide your organization in developing and achieving your vision.

Tools introduced:
- Lewin's Force Field Analysis (Dr. Duxbury suggests the following textbook as a reference for this analysis: "Managing Change: Cases and Concepts, 2nd Edition" by Todd Jick and Maury Peiperl.)

Chapter 10

Practices introduced:

- Asking the question, "Who can I be that my employees' eyes shine?
- Asking how you can create a culture that learns from its mistakes.
- Finding language that helps your teams grow.
- Learning how to facilitate emergent discussions.

Tools introduced:
- EQ In-Action Profile, from Learning and Action Technologies.

Chapter 11

Best advice from the featured influencers:
- Become a transformational leader.
- Shift to a foundation for psychological health.
- Reward what you value.
- Determine your desired state.
- Create a learning culture.
- Be a compassionate leader.
- Initiate conversations.
- Value others.
- Create more space for reflection.

Tools introduced:
- Increasing your integrity and helping others to increase theirs.
- Having a mindset that says, "we have to learn our way through complexity."
- Communicating continuously.
- Effectively dealing with conflict.
- Developing a participatory network methodology.
- Cultivating awareness, understanding and carefulness.
- Assessing the balance between stress and satisfaction in your workplace.

- Using the power of poetry through approaches such as the Poet in Residence program. (www.ronnabloom.com)
- Developing personal awareness.
- The Culture Index from Human Synergistics.
- Defining behaviours that enliven your values.
- Nurturing compassion and positivity.
- Healthy Organization Assessment© Tool. (www.grahamlowe. ca)
- The Neighbour at Work Imperatives, which are a set of evidence-based practices that were conceived and originated by Dr. Shain. They include the following:
  1. GuardingMinds@Work: a strategic approach to improving organizational effectiveness through enhancing the social and psychological wellbeing of its members. The GuardingMinds@Work website provides a self-directed series of free tools including organizational reviews, surveys, reports and strategies to work toward a more psychologically healthy organization. (http:// www.guardingmindsatwork.ca/info)
  2. Vital Workplace©: a programmatic and cultural approach to improving teams and other work units through enhancing the social and psychological wellbeing of their members. Vital Workplace© is a guided process facilitated through the Canadian Mental Health Association in partnership with N@W and is aimed at building, maintaining and restoring a culture of civility, respect and a sense of psychological safety within teams, departments and units. Through this process, the N@W Imperatives can be integrated into your existing offerings, such as Respectful Workplace Policy, anti-bullying programs, and more. (http://www. neighbouratwork.com/vital-workplace.asp)

Other tools recommended by the author

The STORM Index: a cultural assessment tool developed by Dr. Michael Peterson, a past speaker at the Conference. (www.stormindex.com)

Workplace Strategies for Mental Health: an initiative of the Great-West Life Centre for Mental Health in the Workplace, containing free resources to improve the psychological health and safety in your workplace. (www.workplacestrategiesformentalhealth.com)

27 Great Ideas for Positive Practices from Thoughtexchange:

Adding to what the experts above recommend, the organizational health community were asked in our Positive Workplace Culture Thoughtexchange to share positive practices from their own or client workplaces. I chose the top 27 ideas and listed them here. Use them to spark ideas of your own for practices you can tailor to suit your organization.

1. Identify the bright spots. Look at teams elsewhere that report a positive work culture and explore them for ideas.
2. Share the facilitation. Let each employee be the next month employee meeting facilitator. It empowers the notion that everyone is equal in the organization. You feel it!
3. Mentoring programs. With five generations in the workforce, organizations have an opportunity to establish two-way mentoring programs that focus on sharing knowledge and experiences.
4. Have an outside expert leading a workshop on workplace health. It's often helpful to have an expert who is not part of the team highlight avenues and goals to improve cohesiveness, collaboration and respect.

5. Looking for the positive through nominations for recognition programs. Recipients of awards generated through nominations from colleagues feel great knowing that others think highly of them. Those submitting nominations must look for positive aspects within their work life to nominate someone, which promotes positive thoughts and interactions.

6. Recognition toolkits. A Not-For-Profit organization I am involved with recently gave every leader an actual toolkit with recognition resources. Keep it simple!

7. Positive stories on message boards. In lunch rooms, set up a white board where employees can write brief stories about teammates that went above and beyond the call of duty to help other teammates.

8. Daily huddles. A staff member of mine asked for daily meetings, which I initially thought was too much. When we started doing these daily, stand-up "huddles" though, I found that they were short, helped us stay connected and we got through our workload much faster.

9. On-boarding into the culture. A comprehensive on-boarding protocol helps new hires with socialization and assimilation into the corporate culture earlier.

10. Performance management measures that value behaviours and collaboration. If organizations adopt performance management systems that reward positive behavior, the culture in the organization will improve.

11. Measure healthy workplace practices. Don't just focus on lagging indicators like absenteeism and the number of employee relations cases. Measure how often recognition systems are being used. How many potential high performers have you identified? There is an old adage that "what gets measured gets time and attention."

12. Positive cultures start with values-based recruitment and hiring. My experience shows that when companies understand and hire based on the values of their culture versus just on technical skills and knowledge, the culture is more likely to become self-managing and self-sustaining. Couple this with thorough on-boarding, establishing expectations around contributions and what the team member can reasonably receive in return and the organizational culture wins.

13. Giving attention to ongoing discussion about healthy culture. Build in time to discuss your culture at all staff meetings.

14. Tell stories. A current client of mine that has a healthy workplace culture starts every meeting with a positive story about a teammate, client or event that reflects the organization's values. This sets the tone and culture for the meeting. Very simple, and costs nothing!

15. Invest in your culture. Creating a positive culture requires sustained commitment and an investment of time and money. Things that are important to invest in include training and development, coaching and mentoring support, opportunities for face-to-face interaction, recognition programs and ways of measuring progress.

16. Educate top management on "stress culture." Educate top management about the financial consequences of a high-stress culture (busy-ness, multi-tasking, due yesterday, never enough). Help management become more realistic in their expectations, and to realize that it is workers' performance and productivity that make up the organization.

17. Get teams together to talk about their culture and how to improve it. We often don't get together to discuss this because we're too busy doing our jobs. Once we understand through measurement where we're currently at, we can identify areas to work on. This can become a shared focus for the team.

18. Listen into action. Hold forums regularly for all staff to identify challenges they face and be given the authority, skills and resources to deal with those challenges. This empowers all staff, releases innovation and gives a strong sense of control to all staff, helping them to thrive and innovate.

19. Openness and transparency of senior management. I know a senior management team who hold town halls every month to talk about current priorities, issues, future plans, hot topics and to recognize work well done. They are approachable and welcome comments and suggestions, even anonymously, in an effort to continuously improve.

20. Flex hours. In this organization, employees are given a range of time to work. They choose what works for them. Some can drop off kids at school on the way to work. Some pick up kids on the way home from work. Some are not early morning people and can work during their peak hours. In some cases an employee puts in extra time during peak periods and then takes more time off during slow periods. This helps staff balance work demands with family needs and helps them feel valued and respected.

21. Support LIFE-Work Balance. We commonly refer to work/life balance, but as life outside of work encompasses a greater part of who we are, we need to think of this in reverse by recognizing that work is only a part of the life spectrum. People with positive lives outside of work are better employees.

22. Role model how to reduce sedentary time in the workplace. The concept of walking or standing meetings is role modeled and encouraged by leaders in the organization. Sit-stand desks are provided (especially to those that have issues sitting for long periods of time), breaks are taken by leaders and staff are encouraged not to work through their breaks.

23. Regular discussions about the vision and values. Have ongoing process in place to make sure there is a discussion at least annually about the behaviours that support a positive culture. Everyone needs to be able to identify them. Reward people for behaviours that fit with the vision and values.

24. Engage champions to cascade your culture. Champions who embrace the culture you aspire to have, are proven performers and have earned the respect of other staff are incredibly useful in helping to cascade a positive workplace culture. They help harness enthusiasm and capacity for shifting culture and help maintain momentum and continuity.

25. Create positive social interactions. For example, place a board in the lunch room where people can post things about their lives or their work unit (e.g. the birth of a grandchild or a team award). These tend to start positive conversations versus using the lunch room as a place/time to complain.

26. Have a "blame-free" culture. When mistakes are made, they are not seen as opportunities to teach a staff member a lesson by punishing them. Rather, these are conversations to explore what went wrong and how it can be avoided in future. Humans are not mistake-proof. Many mistakes are caused by system issues.

27. Create a culture where it is OK to disagree. We need to disagree to create and innovate. Neuroscience has shown us when we are curious with one another, dopamine is secreted which makes us feel good. Curiosity allows us to stay in conflict, explore and move forward in a way that works.

Speakers from the Conference

This is a list of all the speakers who spoke at the Conferences from 1997 through 2013. They were carefully and thoughtfully chosen for their expertise, and each one of them is a great resource in their area of practice.

**Conference 1997
(Vancouver, BC)**
A.E. Ready
André Russo
Ann Coombs
Ann de Pominville
Barry Cook
Bob Czimbal
Carol Aberdeen
Carol MacKinnon
Carol Power
Chris Johnson
Don DeGuerre
Donald Ardell
Donna Carswell
Ed Buffett
Elizabeth Healey
Errol Walker
Faheem Hasnain
Gail MacDonald
Gina Dingwell
Hae-Sook Sohn
Harry Hubball
Jack Altman
Jan Mears

Jan Mitchell
Jane Auman
Janice Gould
Jean Martin
Jim Norton
Jocelyn Burgner
John Blatherwick
John Frank
Jon Husband
Judy Sefton
June Donaldson
Kendy Bentley
L.J. Bilek
Larry Axelrod
Linda Aylesworth
Linda Naiman
Liz Gildner
Lori Messer
Marie McNaughton
Mavis Gibson
Michael Epstein
Michael Morierity
Michael Peterson
Nan Bennett
Nancy Johnston

Nancy Shames
Nic Tsangarakis
Norma Mossington
Peter Clark
Richard Whaley
Ron Labonte
Russ Kisby
Sharon Tracz
Shirley Sung
Terrence Dalton

**Conference 1998
(Whistler, BC)**
Ahnna Lake
Anda Bruinsma
Angela Daly
Barbra Daigle
Brian Hiebert
Carol MacKinnon
Chris Bradley
Chris Johnson
Dave Randle
David Whyte
Deb Jones (Connors)
Donald Ardell
Doug Wills
Frederick Weston
Glenys Schick
Hugh MacLeod
Ivory Warner
Jack Santa-Barbara
Jane Boyd

John Pepin
Jon Husband
Jon Shearer
Judd Allan
Judith McBride-King
June Preston
Kendy Bentley
Kevin Frederick Nagel
Larry Axelrod
Larry Stoffman
Lawrence Green
Leah Hawirko
Leonie Serman
Lisa Rezler
Lori Hendry
Marg Bellman
Marilee Mark
Marnice Jones
Mary Ferguson-Paré
MaryLou Harrigan
Mavis Gibson
Nancy Turner
Nora Spinks
Patricia Mackenzie
Randy Adams
Ron Labonte
Roy Shephard
Seigfried Malich
Sheron Stone
Susan Levy
Trish Clayburgh
Zoey Ryan

Conference 1999 (Vancouver, BC)

Alex Campbell
Arif Bhimji
Art Salmon
Carol Ann Fried
Carol Hills
Carol Matuskicky
Craig Thompson
Dan Pagely
Danielle Pratt
David Brown
David Whyte
Dawn Burstall
Donna Craig
Glen Colwill
Gloria McKee
Jane Boyd
Jane Jones
John Bailiff
Karl Brysch
Ken Robertson
Kevin F. Nagel
Kim Snider
Lauren St. John
Marianne McLennan
Martin Shain
Michael Peterson
Niki Ray
Nora Spinks
Pat Selmser
Randy Adams

Reverend Douglas Graydon
Robert C. Fellows
Robert Meggy
Robert Sawka
Roy J. Shephard
Sandy Keir
Seonaid Farrell
Sue Pridham
Susanne Bayuk
Tammy Horne
Tammy Robertson
Veronica Marsden
William E. Wilkerson
Victor Dirmfed

Conference 2000 (Toronto, ON)

April Lewis
Barry Malmsten
Beverley Bell-Rowbotham
Bob Karch
Carol Bailey
Carolyn MacLeod
Danielle Pratt
David Gouthro
David Ranham
Dieter Lagerstrom
Donald C. Cole
Doug Cowan
Eduardo Brunetti
Gottfried Mitteregger
Janet Carr

John Yardley
Jorge Cerani
Joyce Gwilliam
Karen Campbell
Ken Webb
Kevin F. Nagel
Kevin Sykes
Kim Snider
Lindsay Webber
Lynda S. Robson
Martin Collis
Melissa Barton
Nancy Zuck
Pamela Garner
Pauline Poon
Ricardo De Marchi
Ron Plotnikoff
Ronald Colman
Roy J. Shephard
Sandy Keir
Sharon Blaney
Tammy Robertson
Toby Yan
Tohsio Yamazaki
Trudy Boyle
Wanda Corns

**Conference 2001
(Calgary, AB)**
Adam Moscovitch
Allan Fein
Anne Schultz

Barb Byers
Barry Chugg
Beverlee Gilmore
Bob Karch
Carol Ann Fried
Catherin McLellan
Christine Dickie
Daniel Gold
Daniel O'Connor
Danielle Pratt
David Watson
Derwyn Sangster
Donald Crane
Francis Lau
Geoff Smith
Geri McKeown
Gottfried Mitteregger
Graham Lowe
Jesai Jayhmes
Jim Cardinal
Jorge Cerani
Kevin Sykes
Kris Ong
Leah Milton
Linda Duxbury
Linda Eligh
Liza Bialy
Lorie Pulliam
Mahara Brenna
Margaret Cernigoj
Martin Collis
Martin Law

Martin Shain
Michael Peterson
Mike Kennedy
Neal Berger
Pater Abrams
Paul Green
Richard Danielson
Robert McMurtry
Ronald Plotnikoff
Seth Serxner
Terry Sullivan
Trudy Boyle

**Conference 2002
(Lake Louise, AB)**
Andrea Jacques
Annalee Yassi
Anne M. Schultz
Camilla Dietrich
Daniel Lopez Rosetti
David Robertson
Deborah Kern
Elaine Jackson
Eoin Finn
Frank Schnell
Fred Holmes
Geri McKeown
Graham Lowe
Henrie de Boer
Jerry Rose
Joan Wade
John K. Yardley

Katharine Weinmann
Linda Spence
Lorraine Bischoff
LuAn Mitchell
Martin Law
Michael Koscec
Michael P. Leiter
Nicholas D. John
Nortin M. Hadler
Olivia McIvor
Patricia Katz
Peter O'Donnell
Petra Hargasser
Ross T. Tsuyuki
Susan Amos
Sylvia Geiss
Tammy Robertson
Trent Dark
Wayne Boss

**Conference 2003
(Gatineau, QC)**
Angéle Bilodeau
Bernd Tenckhoff
Christina Sinclair
Chuck Rowe
Dan Corbett
Dave Borsellino
Denis Garand
Dianne Buckner
Don Bisch
Doug Cowan

Doug Meecham
Elizabeth S.H. Mills
Ghislaine Guérard
Graham Dickson
Health Canada
John Yardley
Joseph P. Ricciuti
Julian Barling
Kelly Blackshaw
Kelly Howey
Kim Snider
Kirsti F. Vandraas
Larry Myette
Linda Spence
Lise Ricard
Lynn Stoudt
Margaret Eckenfelder
Marie Mac Donald
Marion Menge
Marla Jackson-King
Melissa Barton
Michael Peterson
Michéle Parent
Pat Ferris
Peter O'Donnell
Sophe Dubé
Steve Robinson
Susan Cruse
Terrie Conway
Wayne Corneil

**Conference 2004
(Vancouver, BC)**
Alan Low
Angela Downey
Clarence Lochhead
Carole Schwinn
Chris Bonnett
Fadi El-Jardali
Geri McKeown
Gord Johnson
Graham Lowe
Jo-Ann Youmans
Judith Maxwell
Judith Shamian
Karen Seward
Linda Duxbury
Martin Shain
Mike Kennedy
Paavo Jäppinen
Patricia Chuey
Patrick Trottier
Peter O'Donnell
Raymond Lam
Wayne Streiloff

**Conference 2005
(Montreal, QC)**
Amy Hanen
Andrea Jacques
Carol-Ann Hamilton
Catherine McCarthy
Claudine Ducharme

Corinne Smith
Cyril Bendahan
Dale Nikkel
Daniel Atlan
Don Bisch
Estelle Morin
Frances Cortese
Gilles Lebeau
Grady Cash
Graham S. Lowe
Heather Daynard
Jacinthe Tremblay
Jean-Pierre Brun
Jeff Chambers
Jennifer Reed Lewis
Jill Armstrong
Karen Seward
Louise Hartley
Marie Mac Donald
Nora Spinks
Steven A. Grover
Sylvana LeClerc

**Conference 2006
(Vancouver, BC)**
Al Stubblefield
Andrea Parent
Annette Gibbs
Claudine Ducharme
Colleen McKinnell
Craig Thompson
Danielle Vidal

Dave Mowat
Dawn Sidenberg
Debbie Davis
Donna Clark
Elizabeth Smailes
Estelle Morrison
Francois Lagarde
Gottfried Mitteregger
Grant Donovan
Greg Banwell
Jan Mitchell
John Millar
John Yardley
Karen Seward
Larry Birckhead
Marcia Buchholz
Marie MacDonald
Martin Chung
Martin Collis
Maureen Clarke
Michelle Cooper
Michelle Cooper
Nathalie Pasin
Rick Martinez
Rosamund Zander
Stephanie Speal
Suzanne Paiement
Terry "Moose" Millard
Tom Coates
Trudy Boyle

**Conference 2007
(Toronto, ON)**
Alain Marchand
Alain Thauvette
Anna Rizzotto
Annette Gibbs
Annette Patterson
Carla Rieger
Christina Cavanagh
Daphne Woolf
Denny Courrier
Edie Saunders
Elisabeth Ballermann
Eoin Finn
Estelle Morrison
Graham Lowe
Heather Menzies
Heidi Bushell
Hélène Santerre
Irwin Wolkoff
Iva Lloyd
Jennifer deFour
Joe Seguin
Julia James
Karen Seward
Kelly Putnam
Kevin Wong
Linda Chu
Line Vermette
Marie Mac Donald
Marie-Eve Lepage
Martin Chung

Martin Shain
Patricia Katz
Patricia Ryan Madson
Paul Edney
Pierre Durand
Richard Guscott
Rob Sitte
Rosemarie Fondeur Cruz
Sacha Fraser
Sam Calleja
Sophie Dubé
Stephen A. Grover
Suzanne Paiement
Theresa Rose
Victoria Labalme
Yvonne Thompson

**Conference 2008
(Calgary, AB)**
Alan Caplan
Amy Johnson
Andrée Iffrig
Andrew Hume
Annette Patterson
Barry Munro
Billy Strean
Bonnie Fulton
Bronwyn Ott
Bruce MacLellan
Charl Els
Claude Ouimet
Corrine Tessier

Deborah Connors
Diane Kunyk
Donna Schnedel
Doug Awram
Doug Smeall
Estelle Morrison
Fred Heese
Graham Lowe
Heather Beaudoin
Helen Gardiner
Jen Wetherow
John Yardley
Judy Kerling
Karen Kesteris
Karen Seward
Larry Ohlhauser
Leanne Bilodeau
Lori Casselman
Marie Mac Donald
Mary-Lou MacDonald
Michael Koscec
Mike Ryan
Nan S. Russell
Nancy Lowery
Peggie Pelosi
Peter Robinson
Rhona Berengut
Richard Gottfried
Robin Hornstein
Ruth Rancy
Sharon Bronstein
Sheldon Elman

Susan Flaherty
Susi Hately Aldous
Tammy Robertson
Tessa Trasier
Warren Redman
Wendy Poirier

**Conference 2009
(Gatineau, QC)**
Alan Caplan
Andrée Iffrig
Betty Mutwiri
Bob Bayles
Caroline Samné
Charlotte Logan
Danielle Vidal
Diane Champagne
Edgardo Pérez
Fran Pilon
Frédéric Lavoie
Gillian Leithman
Heather Kennedy
Hélène Grandmaître
Ian Percy
Jennifer Elia
Jennifer Walinga
Joel Hershfield
Karen Seward
Kate Carty
Kelly Losak
Larry Birckhead
Leo LeBlanc

Marie Mac Donald
Marie-Helene Pelletier
Mario Messier
Martin Chung
Martin Papillon
MaryAnn Baynton
Merv Gilbert
Olivia McIvor
Petter Legge
Rory Cohen
Sharon Bronstein
Sharon Carne
Sharon Storoschuk
Sholem Prasow
Suzanne Paiement
Tanis Farish
Teresa Scannell
Victoria Labalme
Wendy Poirier

**Conference 2010
(Vancouver, BC)**
Allan Smofsky
Billy Strean
Chris Molineux
Diane Lacaille
Erin Dick
Graham Lowe
Insiya Rasiwala-Finn
Jennifer Hubbard
Jennifer Walinga
Joanna Whalley

John DeHart
Karen Liberman
Karen Seward
Ken Hemphill
Keri Alletson
Lynda Curtin
Mary Ann Baynton
Merv Gilbert
Michael Campbell
Mira Jelic
Natashia Halikowski
Parkash Ragsdale
Peter Melnyk
Rory Cohen
Stan Slap
Stuart Morgan

**Conference 2011
(Toronto, ON)**
Carla Rieger
Debbi Gordon
Estelle Morrison
Janet Young
John DeHart
Joti Samra
Karen Seward
Leslie Brams-Baker
Lori Casselman
Lynda Curtin
Marie-Claude Pelletier
Mario Messier
Martin Shain

Mary Ann Baynton
Maureen McKenna
Mira Jelic
Myra Lefkowitz
Nancy van Boxmeer
Patrice Roy
Patsy Marshall
Rory Cohen
Roy Spence
Sharone Bar-David
Shephen Hammond

**Conference 2012
(Vancouver, BC)**
Alan Fine
Billy Strean
Bonnie Fulton
Catherine Morisset
Dan Bilsker
Michael West
Eric Pfeiffer
Georgina MacDonald
Ian Arnold
Jean-Marc MacKenzie
Jonathan Winston
Linda Brogden
Mark Attridge
Mary Ann Baynton
Merv Gilbert
Nan Russell
Pierre Durand
Robert Quinn

Shamial Sheikh
Steven Hughes
Tammy Robertson
Val Kinjerski
Vince Gowman

**Conference 2013
(Halifax, NS)**
Alan Caplan
Amy Jen Su
Chris Camp
Dave Carroll
Graham Lowe
Georgina MacDonald
Harry Vedelago
Ian Arnold
Janice MacInnis
Jennifer Walinga
Jim Moss
Judith Plotkin
Karen Seward
Leanne MacFarlane
Louise Chénier
Lynn Bailey
Marie Mac Donald
Mary Ann Baynton
Michael P. Leiter
Michael Rouse
Paul MacKenzie
Paula Allen
Sari Sairanen
Sean Slater

Sharon Bronstein
Stephane Grenier
Suzanne Lepage
Thomas Schneberger

References

Chapter 1: Better Way

1. Rosenbluth, H. *The Customer Comes Second, and other secrets of exceptional service.* New York: William Morrow and Company, Inc., 1992.
2. Allen, R.F., Kraft, C., Allen, J., Certner, B. *The Organizational Unconscious: How to Create the Corporate Culture You Want and Need.* New Jersey: Human Resources Institute, 1987.
3. Quinn, R. *Building the Bridge As You Walk On It: A Guide for Leading Change.* San Francisco: John Wiley & Sons, Inc., 2004.
4. Quinn, R. The Positive Organization: *Breaking Free from Conventional Cultures, Constraints, and Beliefs.* Oakland: Berrett-Koehler Publishers, Inc., 2015.
5. Quinn, R. *The Deep Change Field Guide: A Personal Course to Discovering the Leader Within.* San Francisco: Jossey-Bass, 2012.
6. Fredrickson, B. and Losada, M. "Positive Affect and the Complex Dynamics of Human Flourishing." *American Psychology* 60, no. 7 (Oct. 2005): 678-686.
7. Frederickson, B. *Positivity: Top-Notch Research Reveals the Upward Spiral That Will Change Your Life.* New York: Three Rivers Press, an imprint of the Crown Publishing Group, a division of Random House, Inc., 2009.
8. Bungay Stanier, M. *Do More Great Work: Stop the Busywork. Start the Work That Matters.* Markham: Thomas Allen & Son Limited, 2010.
9. Lowe, G., Graves, F. *Redesigning Work: A Blueprint for Canada's Future Well-Being and Prosperity.* Toronto: Rotman-UTP Publishing, 2016.
10. Culver, H. *Give Me A Break: The art of making time work for you.* Vancouver: Friesens, 2011.

Chapter 2: Engage in Practices

11. Stubblefield, A. *The Baptist Health Care Journey to Excellence: Creating a Culture that WOWs!* Hoboken, NJ: John Wiley & Sons, Inc., 2005.
12. Collins J. and Porras J. *Built to Last: Successful Habits of Visionary Companies.* New York: HarperBusiness, 2002.
13. Zander, Rosamund and Benjamin Zander. *The Art of Possibility: Transforming Professional and Personal Life.* Toronto: Penguin Books Canada Ltd., 2000.

Chapter 3: Positively Deviant

14. Spreitzer, G.M. and Sonenshein, S. "Toward the Construct Definition of Positive Deviance," *American Behavioral Scientist* 47, no. 6 (2004): 828.
15. Spreitzer, G.M. and Sonenshein S. "Positive Deviance and Extraordinary Organizing" *Positive Organizational Scholarship: Foundations of a New Discipline.* Edited by Cameron, Dutton and Quinn. San Francisco: Berrett-Koehler Publishers, Inc., 2003.
16. Ardell, D. *The NEW edition of High Level Wellness: An Alternative to Doctors, Drugs and Disease.* Berkeley: Ten Speed Press, 1986.
17. Lalonde, M. *A New Perspective on the Health of Canadians: A working document.* Ottawa: Minister of Supply and Services, Canada, 1974.
18. World Health Organization. *The Ottawa Charter for Health Promotion.* Geneva, Switzerland: WHO; Nov. 21, 1986. Available from http://www.who.int/healthpromotion/conferences/previous/ottawa/en/

19. Grawitch M., et al. "The path to a healthy workplace: A critical review linking healthy workplace practices, employee well-being and organizational improvements." *Consulting Psychology Journal: Practice and Research* 58, no. 3 (2006): 129-147.
20. Sanofi Canada. *The Sanofi Canada Healthcare Survey 2013: Merging Pathways to Sustainable Health.* Toronto: Rogers Publishing Ltd., 2013, 21.
21. Dunn, H.L. *High Level Wellness.* Arlington: R.W.Beatty, Ltd., 1961.
22. National Wellness Institute, www.nationalwellness.org
23. Quinn, R. *The Deep Change Field Guide: A Personal Course to Discovering the Leader Within.* San Francisco: Jossey-Bass, 2012.
24. Quinn, R. *The Positive Organization: Breaking Free from Conventional Cultures, Constrains, and Beliefs.* Oakland: Berrett-Koehler Publishers, Inc., 2015.
25. Duxbury, L., Higgins, C. *Work-Life Balance in the New Millennium. Where Are We? Where Do We Need To Go?* Canadian Policy Research Networks Discussion Paper, available at http://www.cprin.org. 2001.
26. Huffington, A. *Thrive: The Third Metric to Redefining Success and Creating a Life of Well-Being, Wisdom, and Wonder.* New York: Harmony Books, an imprint of the Crown Publishing Group, 2014.

Chapter 4: Organize Positively

27. Cameron, K., Dutton, J., and Quinn, R. *Positive Organizational Scholarship: Foundations of a New Discipline.* San Francisco: Berrett-Koehler Publishers, Inc., 2003.
28. Quinn, R. *The Positive Organization: Breaking Free from Conventional Cultures, Constrains, and Beliefs.* Oakland: Berrett-Koehler Publishers, Inc., 2015.

29. Jones, D. *Celebrate What's Right With the World*. Film available at http://celebratewhatsright.com/film

30. Fredrickson, B. *Positivity: Top-Notch Research Reveals the Upward Spiral That Will Change Your Life*. New York: Three Rivers Press, an imprint of the Crown Publishing Group, a division of Random House, Inc., 2009.

31. The Positive Organization Generator is available online at The Lift Exchange website, http://www.liftexchange.com/generator

32. Grant, A. and Berg, J. " Prosocial Motivation at Work: When, Why, and How Making a Difference Makes a Difference." *The Oxford Handbook of Positive Organizational Scholarship*. Edited by Gretchen M. Spreitzer and Kim S. Cameron. New York: Oxford University Press, 2012.

Chapter 5: Shift Yourself First

33. Quinn, R. *The Deep Change Field Guide: A Personal Course to Discovering the Leader Within*. San Francisco: Jossey-Bass, 2012.

34. Friedman, R. "Working Too Hard Makes Leading More Difficult." *Harvard Business Review*, Dec. 30, 2014, https://hbr.org/2014/12/working-too-hard-makes-leading-more-difficult

35. Brown, B. *Rising Strong: The Reckoning. The Rumble. The Revolution*. New York: Spiegel & Grau, an imprint of Random House, 2015.

36. Maslach, C. & Leiter, M. *The Truth About Burnout: How Organizations Cause Personal Stress and What to do About It*. San Francisco: Jossey-Bass, 1997.

37. Maslach, C. & Leiter, M. *Banishing Burnout: Six Strategies for Improving Your Relationship with Work*. San Francisco: John Wiley & Sons, Inc., 2005

38. Digh, P. The cycles were developed with ideas from Patti Digh. Information on her work can be found at both www.37days.com and www.pattidigh.com.

39. Schwarz, T. *The Energy Project*, www.theenergyproject.com.

40. Friedman, R. "Schedule a 15-Minute Break Before You Burn Out." *Harvard Business Review*, Aug. 4, 2014, https://hbr. org/2014/08/schedule-a-15-minute-break-before-you-burn-out

41. Evans, L. "The Exact Amount Of Time You Should Work Every Day." *Fast Company*, Sept. 15, 2014, https://www.fastcompany.com/3035605/ the-exact-amount-of-time-you-should-work-every-day

42. Bradbury, T. "Why The 8-Hour Workday Doesn't Work." *Forbes*, June 7, 2016, http://www. forbes.com/sites/travisbradberry/2016/06/07/ why-the-8-hour-workday-doesnt-work/#225f48097981

43. Huffington, A. *Thrive: The Third Metric to Redefining Success and Creating a Life of Well-Being, Wisdom, and Wonder.* New York: Harmony Books, and imprint of the Crown Publishing Group, 2014.

44. Kushlev, K., Dunn, E. "Checking Email Less Frequently Reduces Stress." *Computers in Human Behavior*, 43 (Feb. 2015). DOI: 10.1016/j.chb.2014.11.005.

45. Cavanagh, C. *Managing Your Email: Thinking Outside the Inbox.* Hoboken: John Wiley & Sons, Inc., 2003.

46. Friedman, R. "Working Too Hard Makes Leading Difficult." *Harvard Business Review*, Dec. 30, 2014, https://hbr.org/2014/12/ working-too-hard-makes-leading-more-difficult

47. Division of Sleep Medicine. Healthy Sleep, http://www. healthysleep.med.harvard.edu

Chapter 6: Ignite Positivity

48. Frederickson, B. *Positivity: Top-Notch Research Reveals the Upward Spiral That Will Change Your Life*. New York: Three Rivers Press, an imprint of the Crown Publishing Group, a division of Random House, Inc., 2009.

49. Lyubomirsky, S., King, L., and Diener, E. "The benefits of frequent positive affect: Does happiness lead to success?" *Psychological Bulletin* 131, no. 6 (Nov. 2005), 803–855. DOI:10.1037/0033-2909.131.6.803.

50. Quinn, R. *Building the Bridge As You Walk On It: A Guide for Leading Change*. San Francisco: John Wiley & Sons, Inc., 2004.

51. Cameron, K., Dutton, J., and Quinn, R. *Positive Organizational Scholarship: Foundations of a New Discipline*. San Francisco: Berrett-Koehler Publishers, Inc., 2003.

52. Quinn, R. "Positive Emotions and Positive Culture," *The Positive Organization Blog*, June 1, 2016, https://thepositiveorganization. wordpress.com

53. Frederickson, B.L. "Updated thinking on positivity ratios." *American Psychologist* 68, no. 9 (Dec. 2013):814-22. DOI: 10.1037/a0033584.

54. Cameron, K. "Positive Leadership and Extraordinary Organizational Performance." Dean's Lecture Series, Melbourne Graduate School of Education, March 2012, http://education.unimelb.edu.au/__data/assets/pdf_file/0003/.../ Kim_Cameron_pp.pdf

55. Kabat-Zinn, J. *Full Catastrophe Living. Using the Wisdom of Your Body and Mind to Face Stress, Pain, and Illness*. New York: Dell Publishing, a division of Bantam Doubleday Dell Publishing Group, Inc., 1990

56. Langer, E. *Mindfulness*. Woburn, MA: A Merloyd Lawrence book. 1989.

57. Langer, E. *Mindfulness: 25th Anniversary Edition.* Philadelphia: A Merloyd Lawrence Book by Da Capo Press, a member of the Perseus Books Group. 2014.

58. Kabat-Zinn, J. "Mindfulness-based interventions in context: Past, present, and future." *Clinical Psychology: Science and Practice* 10, no. 2 (June 2003):144-56.

59. Kabat-Zinn, J. *Wherever You Go There You Are: Mindfulness Meditation in Everyday Life.* New York: Hyperion, 1994.

60. Tannenbaum, S. and Carasoli, C. "Do Team and Individual Debriefs Enhance Performance? A Meta-Analysis." Human Factors: *The Journal of the Human Factors and Ergonomics Society* 55, no. 1 (Feb. 2013): 231-45. DOI: 10.1177/0018720812448394

61. Kaplan, S., Bradley-Geist, J.C., Ahmad, A., Anderson, A., and Hargrove, A.K. "A Test of Two Positive Psychology Interventions to Increase Employee Well-Being." *Journal of Business and Psychology* 29, no. 3 (Sept. 2014): 367–380. DOI 10.1007/s10869-013-9319-4

62. John Kabat-Zinn's bodyscan meditation can be found online on his website at www.mindfulnesscds.com

63. Another source to listen to Jon Kabat-Zinn's bodyscan meditation is https://youtu.be/DTmGtznab4

64. Quan, W. "Meditation: A Powerful Change Management Tool." White Paper presented at ACMP Change Management, Las Vegas, April 12-15, 2015.

65. Huffington, A. *Thrive: The Third Metric to Redefining Success and Creating a Life of Well-Being, Wisdom, and Wonder.* New York: Harmony Books, and imprint of the Crown Publishing Group, 2014.

Chapter 7 Teams

66. West, M. *Effective Teamwork. Practical Lessons from Organizational Research.* Third Edition. Chichester: The British Psychological Society and John Wiley & Sons, Ltd. 2012.
67. Shain, M. Neighbour At Work Initiative, www.neighbouratwork. com
68. Lyubovnikova J., West, M.A., Dawson, J.F. and Carter, M.R. "24-Karat or fool's gold? Consequences of real team and co-acting group membership in healthcare organizations." *European Journal of Work and Organizational Psychology*, 24, no. 6 (2015): 929-950. DOI: 10.1080/1359432X.2014.992421
69. Tannenbaum S., and Carasoli, C: "Do Team and Individual Debriefs Enhance Performance? A Meta-Analysis." *Human Factors: The Journal of the Human Factors and Ergonomics Society* 55, no. 1 (2013): 231-45. DOI: 10.1177/0018720812448394.
70. Goleman, D. *Emotional Intelligence.* Why it can matter more than IQ. New York: Bantam. 1995.
71. Aston OD Case Study: *Developing high performing teams as a pivotal driver for Perfect Care.* Mersey Care NHS Trust. 2016. http://www.astonod.com/clients/client-stories/ mersey-care-nhs-trust/

Chapter 8: Inspire Psychological Health

72. Shain, M. Stress, Mental Injury and the Law in Canada: A Discussion Paper for the Mental Health Commission of Canada (February 2009), https://www.mentalhealthcommission.ca/ English/media/3043

73. Shain, M. Tracking the Perfect Legal Storm: Converging systems create mounting pressure to create the psychologically safe workplace. May, 2010, https://www.workplacestrategiesformentalhealth.com/pdf/Perfect_Legal_EN.pdf

74. Shain, M. Weathering the Perfect Legal Storm: Navigating requirements of the emerging duty to provide a psychologically safe system of work in the context of the voluntary National Standard of Canada on Psychological Health and Safety in the Workplace CSA Z1003-13/BNQ 9700-803, A Bird's Eye View. 2014. http://www.workplacestrategiesformentalhealth.com/pdf/weathering_the_perfect_legal_storm_BEV_E.pdf

75. Collins, J., *Assembling the Pieces. An Implementation Guide to the National Standard for Psychological Health and Safety in the Workplace*. Developed for the CSA Group and the Mental Health Commission of Canada. 2014. ISBN 978-1-77139—830-5.

76. The National Standard of Canada for Psychological Health and Safety in the Workplace, 2013. https://www.mentalhealthcommission.ca/English/national-standard

77. Shain, M. *Best Advice on Stress Risk Management in the Workplace.* A publication developed for Health Canada, 2000. Cat. No. H39-546/2000E. ISBN 0-662-29236-7.

78. Rousseau, D. "Psychological and implied contracts in organizations." *Employee Responsibilities and Rights Journal* 2, no. 2 (1989): 121-39. DOI: 10.1007/BF01384942.

Chapter 9: Vision

79. Aston OD. The Aston Team Positivity Measure, www.astonod.com

80. Jick, T., Peiperl, M. *Managing Change: Cases and Concepts*. 2nd Edition. New York City: McGraw-Hill/Irwin, 2003.

81. Quinn, R. "When the Vision is a Living Thing." *The Positive Organization*, Aug 10, 2016, https://thepositiveorganization. wordpress.com/

82. Spence, R. It's Not What You Sell, It's What You Stand For. *Why Every Extraordinary Business is Driven by Purpose*. New York: Penguin Group, 2009.

83. Lowe, G. *Creating Healthy Organizations: How Vibrant Workplaces Inspire Employees to Achieve Sustainable Success*. The University of Toronto Press, Toronto, ON (2010).

Chapter 10: Emergent Process

84. Quinn, R. *Building the Bridge As You Walk On It: A Guide for Leading Change*. San Francisco: John Wiley & Sons, Inc., 2004.

85. Brown, B. *Rising Strong: The Reckoning. The Rumble. The Resolution*. New York: Spiegel & Grau, an imprint of Random House, a division of Penguin Random House LLC. 2015.

86. Zander, R., and Zander, B. *The Art of Possibility. Transforming Professional and Personal Life*. Toronto: Penguin Books Canada Ltd. 2000.

87. Quinn, R. *The Positive Organization: Breaking Free from Conventional Cultures, Constraints, and Beliefs*. Oakland: Berrett-Koehler Publishers, Inc., 2015.

Chapter 11: Best Advice

88. Marie refers to Kotter, who's work can be found here: Kotterinternational.com

About the Author

When Deborah went back to university to do her Master's degree in the eighties, she wanted to study organizational health. However, there was no such degree at the time. She was able to find the right advisors and create a program that allowed her to conduct research on health promotion in organizations. She then started her consulting business, Well-Advised Consulting Inc., which provides support to organizations wanting to create more positive and healthy work cultures.

In the nineties, when there was no annual conference in Canada on organizational health, Deborah had the vision to develop the Health Work & Wellness™ Conference (now branded The Better Workplace Conference), a national event that she led for 17 years.

Now she has captured the knowledge and best-advice from an entire community of organizational health professionals, researchers and business leaders that came together annually for her event. She conducted in-depth interviews with ten featured influencers in the organizational health field in order to create "A Better Place To Work: Daily Practices That Transform Culture" and to inspire her keynotes, retreats and in-house workshops.

A captivating speaker, storyteller, author and workplace coach, Deborah researches the latest breakthroughs in organizational health and culture around the globe. She teaches leaders how to radically shift culture so that people can flourish.

Deborah lives on Vancouver Island with her husband Mike and their youngest daughter Jordan. She is happiest when she is on stage teaching or on the mountain skiing with her family.

"Singlehandedly, through the vehicle of her annual conferences, Deborah brought the field of workplace health promotion and wellness to a point where it is now a mature, thriving concept. She saw the industry through its early days of preoccupation with personal health practices and led it skilfully into the more contentious area of organizational health. There is, in short, no other one person in Canada who has done more for the field. As a major thought leader and organizer of the field, I hope that Deb will be our beacon for many years to come."

—Dr. Martin Shain, Principal, Neighbour at Work Centre®

Better Way Engage in Practices

POSITIVELY DEVIANT

Organize Positively

Shift Yourself 1st

Ignite Positivity

TEAMS

Inspire
Psychological Health

VISION

Emergent Process

The BE POSITIVE framework provides over 50 daily practices that support creativity, innovation and proactivity at work. Deborah also offers the following opportunities to create daily practices that transform the culture in your workplace:

Keynotes
Ignite Positivity!
Workplace Practices That Transform Culture

Online Courses
8-Weeks To A Better Place To Work
Join an online community and work together in adapting the practices in "A Better Place To Work: Daily Practices That Transform Culture" to meet the needs in your workplace. It's like a book club with online coaching, meeting weekly to learn and share.

Team Workshops
Positive Teams Transform Culture

Leadership Retreats
Mindful Leadership Practices That Transform Culture

Book Deborah to speak in your organization at contact@deborahconnors.com

Visit Deborah at:

DeborahConnors.com
Facebook.com/WellAdvisedConsulting
LinkedIn: Deborah Connors
Twitter: @Well_Advised
Instagram: deborah.connors